Succeeding as a Student in the STEM Fields with an Invisible Disability

Succeeding as a Student in the STEM Fields with an Invisible Disability

A College Handbook for Science, Technology, Engineering, and Math Students with Autism, ADD, Affective Disorders, or Learning Difficulties and their Families

Christy Oslund

Jessica Kingsley *Publishers*
London and Philadelphia

First published in 2013
by Jessica Kingsley Publishers
116 Pentonville Road
London N1 9JB, UK
and
400 Market Street, Suite 400
Philadelphia, PA 19106, USA

www.jkp.com

Library of Congress Cataloging in Publication Data
A CIP catalog record for this book is available from the Library of Congress

British Library Cataloguing in Publication Data
A CIP catalogue record for this book is available from the British Library

ISBN 978 1 84905 947 3
eISBN 978 0 85700 817 6

Printed and bound in Great Britain

Contents

Introduction

It was a Sunday morning in late August, the air outside was crisp, the sun was shining through leaves that were beginning to turn red. As I opened the main door to my office suite there were already parents waiting outside the door for me. Twenty minutes later as I walked the first set of parents out to the main door, I saw my waiting room was full. Families were stacking up waiting to see me. It was the weekend parents were meant to "drop off" their students for orientation week, or O-week, the introduction to campus where students would gradually be introduced to their new life for the next four or five years. Instead of wandering around campus admiring our flower gardens, or taking part in the family picnic, these people were lining up to see me— the coordinator of student disability services—despite the fact that most of them had faxed me their student's documentation for services months ago. My office was supposed to be open for several hours that Sunday so that parents could stop in and say hello. When I finally closed and locked the office door that evening I had seen a dozen families, the last one for over an hour and a half. Out of all those families one stood out to me because the mother had her student well prepared for the transition he was about to make to life away from her, away from constant support for taking his medication, getting up, keeping appointments, living independently.

By Monday morning as I continued to process what I'd experienced on Sunday, it began to strike me that if one mother stood out for the preparedness of her student, that meant 11 families and students were in some identifiable way underprepared. It was the kind of statistic I didn't have time to dwell on as I took part in presentations and meetings designed to help the students get to know campus, settle in, learn about the range of support services available and otherwise make them comfortable before the returning students arrived. The following week, as classes began, I already had panicked, underprepared freshmen showing up in my office. I expected to see this but not for at least several weeks, usually when first tests were being given.

One young man told me, "I was curled up in the fetal position and crying all day Wednesday last week." Last week—it was just O-week—it was designed to be fun with games, food, and lots of chaperoning by specially trained peer leaders who knew how to make everyone feel included. Yet here was this student, who had made his way into my office by special invitation after thrusting a letter requesting accommodation at the Dean of Students during an O-week activity. When the Dean opened the letter, she'd immediately looked for me and my colleague, the head of counseling services. When the student arrived in my office he was visibly a wreck, disheveled, with eyes swollen from crying, and anxiety wafting off his pale, jittery body as he perched on the edge of a chair.

As we began discussing his situation, I asked him about other times he'd been away from home. He explained, "I've never been away from home for more than a night before."

I thought perhaps he misspoke. "You never went to summer camp..."

"No," he insisted, "I've never spent two nights away from home before. I count on my mother to balance me out when I'm getting too anxious."

I couldn't help but think, "What were your parents thinking when they let you come here? Why didn't they at least send you to relatives or otherwise begin to prepare you for this separation? How does anyone get to be 18 without spending two nights away from home?"

During the first week of classes I continued to meet underprepared freshmen. "How do I remember to take my medicine?" "Who will help me get up for class?" "How do I know what books to buy?" Before Friday I found myself sitting in a meeting with the person in charge of our First Year Programs. I think we had a similar glazed look and I said, "I've never seen so many underprepared students in one place at one time."

She nodded then held her hands up in bewilderment, "This is crazy! We're already swamped and the semester has barely begun." We both expected that some students would feel overwhelmed; many are autistic, have a learning disability, attention deficit disorder, and/or live with anxiety disorders and/or affective disorders. In the past though, we'd made it closer to mid-terms before we saw this level of anxiety amongst our freshmen. If they were like this after less than one week…

When I was working on my doctorate degree, I did research which found the best way to teach someone a new thing is to have him or her practice alongside someone who already knows how to do what the person is learning. I focused on how people learn to write, and on how they learned new ways of writing in school—but my research found the same basic principle applies to learning in general. For example, if you want to learn how to drive a car, you ought to practice with someone who already knows how to drive. It will help you immensely if the person you are learning to drive from has some experience *teaching* others how to drive and has learned how to say out loud things that are normally learned through experience. Rather than letting you first have an accident because you changed lanes without checking your blind spot, this person would say, "Always do a quick glance over your shoulder to check your blind spot before changing lanes."

As I reflected on parents and children who were not ready for the transition to college I realized the same principle was at work. Most parents do not face the exact same challenges their children do—so even if the parents had been to the same college their child was going to attend, they probably didn't realize how best to prepare their child for the transition. Even if the parents did share the same or similar challenges as their child, having never taught another person how to prepare for the transition to college, parents probably weren't able to make a list of everything their child would need to know and do, or be able to talk about these items in detail. It isn't until we try and teach someone a new skill that we begin to think about how to put into words what we have learned from experience. At the same time, the children who were learning might have questions that related to basics like, "Where will I get food?" or "How will I know where to find my classrooms?" but will not know enough about living away from home and studying at college to ask other kinds of questions. And often children are so excited about the change, and anxious, that their question-asking can be very focused on a few things, like how they would get home if things didn't work out or how much notice parents will provide before "dropping in."

It occurred to me that what would help families—both parents and children—would be advice and information from someone who had both prepared for college and who was disabled; it would help if this person also knew something about teaching and realized that knowledge gained from experience has to be said out loud, or written where others can see it because such knowledge is not "obvious" as people sometimes mistakenly think it is. My research has taught me that when we have learned to do things without someone explicitly teaching us, we think that such knowledge is obvious when, really, it took us much trial and error and experience to learn.

I realized I was in a unique position to inform families, making them aware of things I had learned by trial and error.

I am disabled. While I long suspected that I learned differently than others, and while I struggled greatly learning to read and write, and then learning how to read and write the way a graduate student is expected to, I was well into my graduate studies before I was diagnosed. It turned out that I live with a variety of invisible disabilities—that is disabilities that cannot be seen. This makes me like many of the students I work with who live both with invisible disabilities and with more than one disability. In my case an affective disorder is accompanied by obsessive compulsive disorder (OCD), anxiety disorder, and I am dyslexic. Being dyslexic presented a huge obstacle to becoming a successful student as did the headaches and anxiety I live with; I can do a very fine job of creating the perfect environment within myself for a headache by worrying about all the things I have not done exactly the way I think they should be done. This was the best possible preparation for realizing what the students I work with have to go through, particularly when they are completely unprepared for the transition that is necessary when moving from living at home to being independent, and the transition that is necessary to rise to the level of work needed at a competitive college.

I realized that perhaps the best way to help students and families be better prepared was to write down what I knew about this transition. My knowledge comes from not only what I had to do as a student but also from what I see the students I now work with going through on a daily basis. I have attended both liberal arts schools and a STEM university. I have also taught different kinds of writing at both liberal arts and a STEM university. I know from experience that many of the things students need to know for making this transition are similar: how to be responsible for your personal medication; how to prepare for tests; what is reasonable behavior from a professor and what is potentially illegal. Whether you are a student with an invisible disability (or multiple disabilities) or a parent helping a student prepare to attend a competitive university, this book contains advice that you can use to be better prepared.

I write this book, then, speaking to two groups of people: parents of a child who has an invisible disability and to students with disabilities themselves who plan to study at university. Some young people will want to be active participants in preparing themselves for university and will read this book for information and ideas. There are places in the book that you can refer to over and over again, including bulleted lists that you can use to remind yourself of how to carry out or prepare for a specific activity.

Parents can use this book to help themselves realize how to assist their child in being as well prepared as possible for the transition to university. Ideally, a family will use this book together, discussing the necessary skills a child needs and how they will practice learning. If a child is already in university, then this book offers some advice for both families and their students about how to deal with some of the complications they may encounter; generally a child/student does not encounter a complication without sharing their frustration with parents who in turn want to assist in finding solutions. If you got a grade you don't agree with, or your child is complaining about the treatment a professor is showing them, then Chapter 7 explains exactly how to proceed. If remembering to take medication is a problem, then Chapter 2 has ideas for how to create a medication routine.

Differences between STEM and Liberal Arts

I realized that if I targeted my advice to students seeking entrance and a degree from a STEM university, I would be giving advice that would apply to any intelligent student who has not had to study their hardest to maintain good grades. There are some key differences between the two types of school which influenced the title of this book.

Liberal arts universities require more general education courses

Students who attend a liberal arts university should realize they will need to take more reading and writing classes than at a STEM university as there is a greater requirement for non-degree related classes such as social sciences and humanities. There are often a wider range of disabilities found on a liberal arts campus because many such schools offer "quality of life" classes for those who are not interested in obtaining a degree, or who do not plan on having a career after they graduate. STEM schools seldom offer quality of life or ongoing education classes. (They may offer continuing-education classes that pertain to professionals who need to maintain certification.)

STEM students take pride in identifying themselves as "geeks"

STEM students take more pride in identifying themselves as "geeks" and "nerds" than the average liberal arts student, even though intelligent "geeks" are not limited to STEM education. "Owning their geek" means the social climate on the campus of a STEM school is different than at non-STEM schools. In one recent presentation when I asked students to identify some of the differences in popular culture between their high school and our STEM school they identified that here they finally found, "*everyone* knows *Star Trek, Star Wars*, has read *Harry Potter* and *Lord of the Rings,* knows Dungeons and Dragons, has played a role-playing game online…and can quote their favorite characters from anything word for word, line by line." This is how the students describe the popular culture on their STEM campus. If you've ever seen a popular culture representation of this group—for example the US television show *The Big Bang Theory*, then you realize this "geek" identity, and these interests, are somewhat universal amongst STEM scholars and students.

STEM universities attract students who excel in sciences and math; most are very computer literate. These are students who are accustomed to being very successful in school and due to previous success in school these students may never have learned to study.

Career Opportunities

STEM schools tend to be very degree and career-oriented and there is also a difference in outcomes for students who make it through our systems. As a former English and Philosophy major I can assure you there are hundreds of applications for every English or Philosophy job that opens and many people who hold PhDs in English and Philosophy are working in jobs for which they are educationally overqualified. STEM schools have higher placement rates for those who successfully graduate with a degree—96 percent of students at my current institution either go to work, to graduate school, or enter the armed services as an officer. Amongst those who go to work, average starting salaries are in the high $50K/£32K range. This is not a "right to try" school[1]; those who enter have GPAs (Grade Point Averages) in the 3.6+ out of 4 range, many having taken advanced placement classes, and early entry college classes, while still in high school.

Mandatory Classes and Educational Expectations

At the STEM school where I currently work there is not much of an expectation to be able to write well by the time the student graduates. While students believe we are trying to "sneak" English classes by them in the guise of university-wide general education classes, students here *can* graduate having taken just one real English/ writing class, plus a few general education classes with limited writing components. Students here refer to their general education courses that require them to write a paper as "English classes" and I just shake my head every time they say this. Many of our students consider writing their personal weakness and believe that having to write a two-page paper every ten days is rather demanding.

At the same time, most are capable, even strong writers who complain they lack confidence in writing because they have had

---

1   "Right to try" refers to institutions that accept students who might not appear otherwise qualified. The student has one probationary semester to prove he can be successful; if his grades are not acceptable at the end of the semester then the student is dismissed. If he has been successful however, the student is removed from probationary status.

too little practice with short essays. They often do not enjoy writing because they do not feel they can do it well and these are students who expect themselves to do everything well.

Professors

Issues of preparedness amongst students thus include needing to reach a level of emotional self-reliance, and physical preparedness to carry out basic life skills, some educational background that families could practice at home, if sufficient preparation is not being offered in the classroom—issues that an increasing number of students setting off for any college or work training opportunity face. STEM education places more emphasis on being prepared in these areas because we also have different professors teaching our classes than you will often find in a liberal arts school.

Again, based on educational and life experience I would say that affective disorders like bipolar and unipolar disorder are spread fairly evenly amongst faculty on all campuses. When it comes to STEM fields however, there is a higher concentration of the autism spectrum disorders, with a concentration of high-functioning autism spectrum disorders or Asperger's syndrome not only in our students but also in our faculty. Anecdotal information based on conversations with other disability service providers at national conferences indicates that the only schools with a higher concentration of Asperger students or faculty are those that focus strictly on computer programming and program design. Whether or not someone is autistic, the overlap between anxiety, obsessive compulsive disorder, high intelligence, and distractibility combined with an ability to focus in myopic detail on highly specialized data, can be found on every STEM campus, again probably in even more concentrated numbers amongst the faculty than amongst the students.

The same things that can set off the students that attend our school can upset the professors: perceived disrespect, unclear communication, and breaks in routine are all fodder for unpleasant encounters between students and faculty. At the same time, anyone involved in education can probably talk your ear off regarding the ways social media, tweeting, instant messaging, role-playing games, etc. have changed (1) the students' ability to discern the difference between an informal interaction and a formal one, (2) the students' lack of practice with formal communication, (3) students who have not learned how to respectfully write an email, or make a telephone call that is contextually appropriate to someone who is not their peer. Imagine having an anxious student interrupt a professor who is equally anxious to return to research, in order to demand a service that the professor is not institutionally expected to provide. Even if someone else does provide that service on campus, not all professors are prepared to take the time to explain this to a student. Knowing where on campus to go to ask different kinds of questions is exactly the kind of preparation many students lack.

Notes About Language Used Within this Book
University and College
I use the terms "university" and "college" interchangeably. While there is some movement for the term "college" to refer to a regional school that does not grant four-year degrees, this is not by any means yet universal. Therefore, a child may start at a college that does grant four-year degrees or a university that is regional rather than drawing from a national or international population as their student body. It is increasingly common for students to use a combination of college and university to obtain a degree. Both are valid places to study and I do not wish to privilege one over the other, so I use the terms interchangeably. There are a few places, however, where I will speak specifically about "community colleges,"[2] and what I say about community colleges is just as applicable to a smaller, regional university, that is, they are places where a student who intends to graduate from a larger school can begin their studies, even if the student has every intention of attending a different school to complete her studies.

Him and Her, He and She
English is such an imperfect language that it provides no term to speak of an individual that does not imply a gender. I can talk about him, or her, and it is clear that I am speaking of one person. If I

---

2   In this case "community college" refers to an educational institution that focuses on two-year programs that students take before transferring to a four-year degree granting institution; these schools also offer technical certifications.

say "them" or "their" then it sounds like I am talking about multiple people. Thus if I want to write a sentence that says, "your child is not likely to get through school without having to talk to at least one of his/her professors" I have to say "his/her" to be grammatically correct and still include both genders. I find this rather tedious and as a reader I find it tedious when a writer does this, even when I understand why he/she is doing so. I will therefore do here what we are starting to do in academic journals. I will switch back and forth between talking about you or your child as "he" and "she" or "him" or "her." I am not implying that you or your child's gender is changing or uncertain—although for some families that may be the case. I am simply using an imperfect language to attempt to equally imperfectly talk about a range of people. I hope you can bear with me through these jumps in gender identity which are built into the language when one wishes to be inclusive.

A Note about Me Professionally and Academically

Professionally I am a member of the Association on Higher Education and Disability (AHEAD) the professional association for disability services providers at the college/university level. I have virtually always been part of the disabled community; I began working as a junior counselor at camps for the disabled when I was ten but was spending my summers in my parents' company at such camps from the age of four. My parents, now retired, specialized in what was known as "special education." My mother, a registered nurse, and my father, a speech and language pathologist, used to work summers at camps for disabled children; during the school year my dad worked for the school district, traveling amongst the schools within a district to work with children. It came as a surprise to me as a young adult to find that many people didn't know much about disabilities or the disabled—I hadn't realized that people grew up isolated from this kind of diversity and knowledge.

While living with undiagnosed dyslexia and an affective disorder as well as several associated disorders, I have completed my BS, MA, MFA, and PhD. The struggles I faced accomplishing this has left me with a passion for improving educational environments for younger people—I am a proponent of decreasing the number of handicapping physical and contextual conditions present in the educational environment.[3]

I welcome your family to make use of this as a reference book that will provide what I consider the "insider information" that one usually has to obtain through experience, trial and error. Ideally it will help you prepare for the transition to college, or to better deal with university if you or your child are already there. I also look forward to hearing from many of you and perhaps meeting some of you in the future as you progress on your individual paths. Perhaps my greatest sense of personal achievement comes from the fact that I have finally arrived at a point where I am able to mentor young people who face their own struggles and that, on occasion, I am able to provide some insight or advice that aids them. If nothing else, I have been able to provide a listening ear when students need to vent their frustration about the difficulties they are facing. I am constantly reminded that listening and offering encouragement are of vital importance; human beings are social despite our disabilities and we tend to benefit when we know another human takes an interest in our progress. I have no doubt that the students I am able to mentor now will grow to become mentors in their own time. I trust that the student-readers of this book will also become mentors in their own right one day. It is my privilege to offer some information which might help you achieve your personal goals.

---

3   "Universal Design" is the formal name for the concept that we design spaces and, in the case of education, classes and lesson plans, so that people with as many learning styles and capacities as possible can participate and demonstrate what they are learning.

1

The Importance of Self-Reliance

My aunt had been teaching high school English for a number of years but recently it seemed that the increasing amount of paperwork she was required to do was sucking the joy out of her career. "You know, they have a rule now that I have to post all my assignments online, including my daily lesson-plans, so that parents can see what we're doing every hour of the day in class. Ditto for current grades—parents want access to that information online, 24/7."

Internally I was relieved I had not taken her earlier advice; I had refrained from becoming a high school English teacher myself and the more she told me about her job the gladder I was not to be sharing a similar position. The longer I'm in my current role as a disability service provider at a STEM university though, the more I realize that parent expectations from high school are carrying over into the rest of their students' lives. Parents increasingly expect to know what their students are doing at all times, what their grades are, how professors arrive at the grades they do, and overall, who on campus is responsible for insuring their students' wellbeing once the parents themselves drive away from campus. In some cases parents want to continue being involved on the micro-level even after their sons and daughters graduate university and accept employment. In *The Trophy Kids Grow Up*, Ron Aslop explains that some parents have gone so far as to show up at job interviews with their now adult offspring.[1] For those of us who grew up in an age when parents still

---

[1] Aslop, R. (2008) *The Trophy Kids Grow Up: how the milleniual generation is shaking up the workplace.* San Francisco, CA: Jossey-Bass.

dropped students at the dorm and then drove home to remodel the student's former bedroom into a lounge, or rent it out, this may seem surprising…until we step back and look at the expectations we have for involvement in our own children's lives. As one colleague shared, "I get so irritated when I'm explaining to a parent that we can't give them all that private information they want…then my daughter had a hard time with a professor in class and I wanted so badly to call him up and ask him what he was doing!"

Parents raising children with disabilities have often had to be strong advocates during their student's schooling process and it is understandable that they expect ongoing involvement with their children's future. If it wasn't for parents advocating for their disabled children, many of these students would never have had the opportunity to be mainstreamed and many children would not have had the opportunity to realize their potential. Their parents' active involvement in every aspect of their education and development has made a real difference and I expect it to be more difficult for these parents to realize when it is time to start transitioning their children towards greater independence. In a society where parents in general are tending to be increasingly involved with their children's day-to-day choices and many children arriving at university are dependent on guidance from their parents, it is ever less likely that the parents of disabled children are going to realize the importance of a level of independence for their son or daughter before that student leaves for university. It is thus not uncommon for the young people drawn to education in science, math, engineering and technology to be very intelligent but to lack some of the coping or problem-solving skills that will help them be successful adults.

Many of the "invisible" disabilities—like autism spectrum disorder, affective disorders, ADD, OCD, LD, dyslexia, and anxiety disorder—make it difficult for a student to look beyond specific smaller details to make long-term plans. Focus, high levels of anxiety, difficulty maintaining good time management practices, even encountering new situations can be very stressful for students with this range of disabilities. Their stress levels in turn can stop students from functioning. In my work I too often encounter young people whose response to being overwhelmed is to start shutting down. They quit turning in homework even when they are doing it; they start missing meals; they start sleeping through classes; eventually they quit going to class and may even stop leaving their dorm rooms. All students benefit from practice making and putting into practice independent decision-making skills *before* they arrive at university. For invisibly disabled students, achieving a level of self-reliance before they arrive on campus often makes a difference between who will survive, thrive, and graduate.

It may help families to understand the importance of practicing self-reliance before their student arrives at university, if they first understand some of the key differences between high school and university. Some of these differences are legal, some are practical but all will require a level of independence that many invisibly disabled students will not achieve without practice and mentoring. These practices, put into place before a student leaves for university, will dramatically increase the probability of the student having a successful transition to their new school and eventual career.

Changes in Legal Status and Rights

I will use US federal law as an example of how a student's status changes once they enter university. Under the Family Education Rights and Privacy Act (FERPA) it is illegal for university faculty and staff to share information about a student with anyone, including parents, unless:

- The student has signed a waiver of the right to privacy.

- The student has clearly identified what kind of information may be shared.

Students can choose to only share billing information, and/or final grades with parents and must specifically agree in the waiver that parents are allowed access to personal information beyond grades and bills.

Parents may be paying the bills but students still have the legal right to limit the information parents receive. And while most parents insist that their students do show them the grades at the end of the semester, students have the legal right to withhold this information even if their parents do pay the bills. No more report cards, no more status reports during the course of the term; even if professors are called they are legally prohibited from sharing information about a student with anyone. Not only will professors not tell you how your student is doing in their class, calling the Dean of Students' office, or the Chancellor, is not going to get parents any further information. Universities *can state* that a student is not currently enrolled with them but this is a question that parents never seem to ask—we've had more than one family bring a student to school only to find out at the end of the semester that the student immediately dropped out of classes but remained in town. Nor are we the only school to have had parents show up for graduation only to discover that their student stopped attending classes some time ago.

This does not mean that the university is uninterested in the student's welfare. Many campuses now have their own version of what on our campus is called the Early Intervention Team (EIT). On our campus this committee is made up of representatives from Counseling Services, Conduct Services, Housing, the International Students' office, the Dean of Students, Financial Aid, and the head of Police and Public Safety. EIT meets every week and if anyone in any department has a reason to be concerned about a student they know to bring this student to the attention of a member of the EIT team. Once a student is raised in EIT, someone on the committee will be responsible for doing an informal wellness check on the student. This will include checking for any reports from the resident advisor (RA) who lives on the student's floor, asking for updates from the student's faculty, and seeking information from any other service providers the student may have reason to come into contact with. If the student receives disability services then EIT will want to know about my interactions with the student—whether I have seen them recently or have any concerns. None of this information however, is available to parents. We only alert parents in cases where we feel the student is potentially in danger—a harm to himself or others. We don't call parents if we think a student is likely to fail a class; as an adult the student is allowed to choose to fail by not responding to offers of help or by simply not doing what is expected of him.

We will reach out *to the student* if we identify a reason for specific concerns about her—be it her lack of attendance in class or her overall demeanor. If the student is already working with me, then I will email her and ask her to come in and meet with me as soon as possible. I often invite students in for what I call "check-in meetings" just to see how they are managing during the semester. Again though, I do not discuss these meetings with parents. This is one of the reasons it is so important for students to have the ability to (1) make and keep appointments, (2) be able to advocate for themselves if they are struggling. While a university may reach out to a student when someone has concerns about a student's class attendance, work, or demeanor, no one is going to make a student get up and go to class, go to counseling, or study. The student needs to be able to respond to efforts to reach out to her, be able to work with a service provider on campus, and be able to make decisions without a parent present. For most students, disabled or not, these are skills that need to be learned and practiced before they arrive on campus. It can be an unmanageable learning curve to expect a student who has never made his own appointment to recognize he needs help, make an appointment with a service provider, and then follow through by going to meetings or changing his study habits. Assistance is only as helpful as a student's ability to follow through on what is offered. When students have no experience using services without in effect a parent's constant reminder, then the parents will usually not find out until the end of the first semester just how badly their student is transitioning. Failing grades from a previous honor-roll student can be a rude awakening for a family. I have worked with a number of families who realize at that point that their student needs a lot more practice being independent enough to follow up on support. We are then all left scrambling trying to prepare a student to have more success before he is told he has to leave the university due to lack of sufficient progress towards a degree.

In the US the federal laws that parents of disabled students tend to be most familiar with are the Americans with Disabilities Act (ADA) and Section 504 of The Rehabilitation Act. These are the laws that have provided protection to their child so that she has fair and equal access to education. The responsibilities of educators to students, however, changes between the kindergarten to Grade 12 (K-12) system and college/university. While all educators are responsible for opening their classroom to disabled students, once a student leaves the K-12 system, the kind of "equal" access to education she is entitled to changes.

A university is not allowed to discriminate. Not on the basis of age, race, gender, disability, sexual orientation, religion, or political affiliation. No university, however, is responsible for educating everyone who lives within their geographical region. Students must apply for the right to attend any university and each university has a set of reasons they use for taking some people as students and turning others away. Being willing to pay the admittance fee is generally not sufficient to get your son or daughter a seat in a class. For high-functioning, invisibly disabled students the challenge is generally not getting a seat in a class, as they usually have the kind of grades universities are looking for. The fact that a family is paying the bills, however, will not *keep* that seat in a class—students can be and are dismissed for breaking rules of conduct, getting low grades, or failure to obtain enough satisfactory credits to earn a degree. At the university I currently work for failure to pass a set number of credit hours, or maintain a two-point GPA (grade point average) on a four scale[2], will result in a student being on academic probation. Academic probation is a warning. It lets a student know that he is not working to the standard the university expects and that he has one semester to improve his grades. If he does not improve during the next semester, then he faces academic suspension. It does not matter to our institution, or most others, if a family is willing to pay for a student to have the right to keep trying; we will not keep a student who is continuing to underperform in classes. This can be very frustrating for families, even more so when their students are exceptionally bright but for other reasons are failing to maintain at least a C average in classes.

This is one reason why it is so important for a student to arrive able to (1) understand when she needs further assistance to be successful in class, (2) to follow through on support services that are available. The fact that a student is intelligent will not keep her in classes if her grades are poor. Again, this is very frustrating for families. Knowing that a student is intellectually able to do well is not the same as the student having the ability to live successfully away

---

2   In the US and Canada, a 4-point scale is used where each letter grade is worth points, i.e. A = 4, B = 3, C = 2. This system provides some flexibility for differences between institutions in how letter grades are given. For example, some schools do not give A- or B+; others do. Adjusting everything to points makes it easier to evaluate the academic standing of an individual student when she applies for admission.

from home. The legal responsibility of educators at the university level has shifted from that of K-12 educators; we are responsible for educating students who are "otherwise qualified" to pass a class. As a service provider, I can make sure the institution is giving the student extended test time, a non-distracting test environment, or other disability-appropriate accommodations. The institution however, will not change the level or type of knowledge the student must demonstrate he is gaining from the class (nor is it required to by law). If a professor is testing memory—perhaps a pre-med class is being tested on having memorized the parts of the body—no student will be allowed to bring a memory aid like a diagram with all the body parts labeled, into the test.

Disabilities have various effects on what a person is best and least suited to do. Someone with serious impairment to their memory is not well suited to becoming a surgeon because they will not be able to stop and consult reference material while they are performing surgery. While K-12 education has a legal mandate to provide as similar as possible an education for all students, university does not. It may therefore be necessary for students and families to recognize that the area of study that a student believed was his future—perhaps electrical engineering—may not be where his greatest strengths lie. It may at times be necessary for a student to transfer from one department and field of study to another, in order to find where the strengths that he has will be put to best use. Someone interested in medicine but with serious memory limitations might not be a surgeon but may be able to pursue medical research, where reference material and written reminders are feasible adaptations. Self-reliance must be combined with a level of practicality in order for a student to be successful in university.

Real Life Example of the Difference Independence Makes

Several years ago I began working with two young men who were in the same entering class. Both were dyslexic, both were runners on the track team, and both initially registered as engineering majors. Neither was academically successful during their first semester which meant that both would be on academic suspension from competing in track meets. I met with each in turn and we discussed where their real capacities and interests lay. Each conversation revealed underlying facts that foreshadowed the fates of these young men.

The first young man (we'll call him Robbie) confessed that he had no interest in being an engineer. "From the beginning I wanted to go into the sound design program. I love music; it's really all I'm interested in except for running." Why was he registered in engineering? "My dad thought it was a good field for me to study. He doesn't think music is a career."

When I asked Robbie what he was interested in doing differently he had no ideas. The only thing he insisted on was that the running track was important and he wasn't prepared to give it up. His parents both made independent phone calls to me, they insisted that more be done for Robbie and that he had to be on the track team because he valued this activity.

When I talked to the second young man, Stuart, he had a vaguer reason for entering as an engineer. "I thought engineering sounded really interesting. I like to work with my hands…"

When I asked Stuart what he was prepared to do differently, he responded that he was willing to do what was needed to be successful. We agreed that would probably mean a change in majors, as he was already realizing he had no underlying interest in or capacity for engineering. He also agreed he would have to participate less in track and spend more time in learning centers that would support greater academic success within his classes.

Robbie's difficulties becoming a sound design major were compounded during his first semester due to the poor academic results he had; his grade point average was now too low for him to transfer into the program, even if he could convince his father that he needed to make this change. Stuart meanwhile needed to find a department that he could work with where his more serious level of dyslexia would be better accommodated than it was in engineering. Stuart remained flexible about discovering what he might be eventually passionate about studying while Robbie continued to hope for a future in sound design without actively moving towards that goal.

Stuart was better prepared to be independent by his family before he arrived on campus. Unlike Robbie's family, where the father called regularly and insisted that he would pay for extra tutoring if someone could just force-feed his son facts, Stuart's family had been transitioning him to be an independent advocate for services. Stuart had been taught to follow through on meetings. Stuart and his family were also much quicker to accept the fact that being on the track team was detrimental to Stuart's academic future. While Robbie's mom called and pleaded with both the track coach and myself that Robbie not be removed from active participation on the team due to his grades, Stuart stoically resolved to follow the advice he was given and switched to morning runs that were with the team but not for competitive purposes; he stopped attending track meets and all other practices; and he invested time into retaking a few key classes to improve his GPA.

Despite his parent's protests Robbie was not allowed to participate as a member of the track team. Robbie's family emotionally and financially supported his ability to continue to travel to competitions to offer moral support and he continued to run with the team during all practices. His grades did not improve and he switched majors, still not able to get into the sound design program he wanted. Stuart, on the other hand, began to use another of the support services on campus I recommended him to, in this case, the Academic Advisor for Undeclared Students.[3] This academic advisor has a great deal of experience working with intelligent young people who enter a STEM university in a major they are not well suited to. After taking some further aptitude tests Stuart decided to transfer to the Forestry Department. He and I discussed the one great obstacle he still faced— reading, memorizing, and recognizing the variety of plants and trees he would need to be able to identify. Stuart and I discussed the importance of disclosing how dyslexia impacted his ability to spell and memorize with his Forestry professors when giving them the accommodation letters my office provided him with. His professors in turn recognized that the important factor was Stuart's ability to correctly identify plants, not his inability to correctly spell their names. As I write this, Stuart is happily entrenched in Fall Camp, a semester out at the Forestry Center's isolated study center where he is out every day in the field working hands-on. He loves what he's

---

3   In many North American universities it is possible for a student to gain initial entrance without having declared a major/field of study, due to the similar nature of first-year classes that all students must take; students then have at least one semester to identify which field they intend to pursue.

doing, spending time outside and not having to sit at a desk and pore over reading. He has found a new group to be part of and has realized that track is not a sport he is ever going to be competitive in while finishing his degree. He still runs for fun.

Robbie is currently on medical leave from school. The stress of trying to be successful at areas of study that he has no interest in has taken a toll, particularly since his grades have not been good. We have a plan in place should he choose to return. This will include him becoming an Undeclared major, retaking a few key classes to improve his grade standing, and taking a class in sound design without being registered as a sound design major. I'm not sure that Robbie is going to return though. He has found a job working as a disc jockey, he has started writing music with a friend, and this past summer he and his friend were paid for one of their songs. It was not Robbie's dyslexia which got in the way of getting a degree:

- Robbie was not encouraged to be self-reliant.

- He was not allowed to choose his own career goals.

- He was encouraged to pursue interests that were not academic but which negatively impacted his academic performance.

These combined factors did not serve anyone's interests well.

Stuart on the other hand:

- was encouraged to be self-reliant

- was capable of making difficult choices

- was able to be flexible enough to make new goals and independent enough to follow through on specific actions that achieved these goals.

Stuart is on track to graduate with a degree.

Of course, there is no guarantee that both young men will or will not have fulfilling lives after college. As an educator though, I can definitely see that an advantage is given to students who have families that have prepared them to make independent choices and, further, have taught their students how to follow through on actions that lead to achievement. Wishing will not make something happen and we can no more wish success then we can wish away our disabilities.

Practical Considerations for Self-Reliance

Self-reliance does not just better prepare students for the classroom. It can make a dramatic difference in a student's ability to keep himself safe and healthy. I personally have a high threshold for crisis and the life-events I assist students with on a regular basis seldom reach what I would consider a crisis level. A student who nearly dies due to an inability to recognize he needs health care is, however, what I would consider a crisis resulting from a lack of self-reliance. There is a difference between being stoic, and being so used to having someone else be responsible for one's personal health that one is not able to keep oneself healthy. We very nearly lost a young man this past year because he had not practiced the level of self-reliance necessary to seek out medical aid when he was feeling ill, even as the illness became life threatening. His inability to act independently nearly led to tragedy.

I had been working sporadically with this young man, who had issues including attention deficit disorder. His parents were well intentioned but had continued to be responsible for not only making appointments for this young man, but also making sure he followed through and attended appointments. In fact, the only reason this young man initially met with me was because his mother made the appointment and then brought him to the appointment. He had no practice in the practical skills related to caring for his own health needs; he did not keep track of his own prescriptions and did not make his own doctor's appointments. Sometime after he arrived on campus he began to feel ill and during the semester he did nothing about this. He did not call a doctor. He did not walk into the walk-in clinic that is on campus. He decided if he wasn't feeling better by Spring break, he would have his mother make a doctor's appointment for him and take him to the doctor's office. Fortunately for this young man, when one night he became delirious and nonsensical, other students in his dorm rushed him to the emergency room. Tests revealed that during the course of the school year the young man had become a Type I Diabetic and his sugar levels were so high that he was on the verge of coma or death. Given his high numbers the medical staff was amazed he survived without serious complications to any of his organs.

As he lay in his hospital room connected to machines, his mother and I met to discuss his future. We agreed that he needed a lot more practice being independent and that he needed a more supported transition from home-life to independent living. This transition would be better served by first attending a local college, where even if he was living on campus his parents would better be able to make sure he was learning to manage his diabetes. He needed supported practice taking responsibility for his medical and other needs, including practice making and keeping appointments. In this case we agreed he probably would at first need reminders but his parents had to be very conscious of the need to make him start taking responsibility for his own medical treatment—he had to call the doctor, he had to get his prescriptions filled, he had to monitor his diet and insulin level. He obviously was not yet ready to recognize that his own need for medical attention was as pressing as it was. We discussed that he would probably also have trouble recognizing when he would need other support services like meeting with a counselor who could help him learn how to make and keep track of schedules and appointments. It was now much clearer to his mother though, the kind of independence she needed to be teaching and guiding her son towards.

The students most likely to be drawn to STEM education are intellectually high functioning; this doesn't mean they have a number of practical skills or practice carrying out mundane functions like shopping, doing laundry, or even recognizing they are in need of personal hygiene maintenance. When we add in factors like trouble with focus, lack of attention to "unimportant details," and an inability to read social cues, these are not always the students best prepared to immediately move from a supported home environment to an independent environment like a university campus. Transitioning through a local community college or regional university that is not as specialized as the STEM university they intend to graduate from may not be a popular choice with the student but it can be a very useful and practical choice. For the students with the biggest transition to make—those who struggle with maintaining daily schedules, who are still learning to take medicine without reminders, or who are socially very uncomfortable—living at home for a semester or first year of college can allow their established support network to continue working with them. A student who has never taken medication without reminders and has never gotten up on time by herself, cannot be expected to suddenly develop these skills just because she has been geographically relocated. Such students might benefit from first practicing these responsibilities in lower-risk environments like the home environment, where there is still some oversight.

College and Regional Universities as a Transition

For those students who have some of these skills but who may still struggle with independent choices or who have little practice being away from home, a school closer to home allows practice with being independent at a distance that still allows family to physically check in. Some families and transitions are best served by beginning with the student being at a close enough distance to travel home several times during the semester, or for parents to be able to drive to campus should they become concerned about their student.

During our most recent freshman semester, I have communicated with three families who were a long day's drive from campus and yet, the parents became so concerned about their students that they literally jumped into their cars and started driving. They arrived on campus to find there was little they could do short of talk face to face with their student and provide some encouragement. The "emergencies" that drew them here included a student who was not getting up for classes, a student who was depressed being away from home for the first time, and a student struggling to remember to take medication and thus not able to focus in class. If a family has yet to transition from the point where both student and parents are best served by face-to-face communication, then beginning the students' university career closer to home makes sense.

Keeping a student physically closer for a semester or year of transition also makes sense if the student has no practice spending time away from home. Just needing to move can be a traumatic transition—adding difficult classes, new food, being surrounded by strangers, the constant presence of industrial lighting, changes in climate, new smells and experiences can prove to be too much at once for a number of differently disabled young people. Having a few constants in life, whether that be the ability to stay in their own bedroom, or being close enough to home to get home cooking and have geographic familiarity with an area, can make the transition more successful. Some students greatly benefit from this kind of transition by stages; first to college, then to a further distant, even more challenging STEM university.

There is something to be said for beginning a university education at the school one intends to graduate from, particularly if the institution has a robust First Year Program, which actively works at helping students feel part of campus life. A student gets to meet people during their first year, some of whom they will end up graduating with, and friendships can potentially develop from freshman year. That said, there are probably even more reasons why many people are not best served by jumping straight from high school to a highly competitive STEM campus. At this point it is worth mentioning the reality that even if one enters school with a group of students, many are going to switch majors, some will leave school, and new people will continue to arrive during the next few years. Relationships with others will change over the course of obtaining a degree, no matter where one starts their college career and where one graduates from.

The other factor I always remind students of is that no matter where they start— community college, regional university—if they graduate from this STEM university then that is what their degree will say. I encourage students to be more invested in trying to find a co-op[4] or internship before they graduate, than in where they start their initial semester(s) of study. Potential employers will be interested in real life work experience far more than they care about the fact that you spent time in community college. If a different school has the circumstances to help a student make the transition to college successfully, then that is a school worth strongly considering. Parents who are still working on helping their students be semi-independent when it is time to leave high school would be well advised to seriously consider the merits of starting their student at a close-to-home college or university. Students need to practice self-reliance before they are left to fend for themselves.

---

4   A co-op is an opportunity to work hands-on with a company. Co-ops can be arranged as part of a class so that while the student is not paid for their work, they are given academic credit for the experience they gain.

2

Necessary Life Skills for University

The mother on the other end of the phone line was making sure all her bases were covered before her son arrived on campus in three months. We'd been talking about his dorm room and food plan; the conversation was going smoothly until she said, "Just two more things, who will be getting him up and who will make sure he takes his medicine...will that be his resident advisor or the campus nurse?"

I can think pretty fast, which meant that there was only a slight pause as I tried to find the most polite way to respond. "I'm glad you asked that. Since Tim won't be arriving for three months you will have time to start practicing with him. Once he gets here he's going to be expected to get himself up and be responsible for his own medicine." I decided I had better let that sink in before I explained that there was no campus nurse and RAs are never allowed to be responsible for another student's medication.

In high school, staff and faculty may share some responsibility for assisting students with personal care items and some students will even have had personal aids which their school district paid for. This all ends once they enter college. Legally and practically, a university must treat a student as an independent adult capable of making choices and following through on actions that lead to outcomes. A student who does not get up and go to class is seen has having made the choice to sleep in. When a student's disability and perhaps even medication interfere with a student getting up in the morning, then the student is expected to make choices that will offset the disability's impact. So for example, if a student is a narcoleptic, or

AD/HD and taking medicine which causes sleep, then they would be expected to adapt a technology and/or routine to offset the impact of their disability and medication. I work with at least three narcoleptic students: all take medication to keep them alert during the day, two have beds hooked up to machines that shake them awake in the morning, all are expected to maintain a balanced schedule that has them going to bed and getting enough hours of sleep so that they are physically able to function the next day. I work with over a hundred AD/HD students: virtually all are on medication, all are expected (by the university) to maintain a balanced schedule, most work with counseling services and/or academic support services to continue building their scheduling and time management skills.

Some students do need to be on medication that has strong enough side-effects that their accommodations take into account that there are certain hours when they will not be functioning well. I am working with several students who currently have the accommodation of not starting exams any later than 5:00 in the evening, so that they can finish their exams before their medication wears off. Considering that during end of term, exams here can start as late as 8:00 p.m. this accommodation is important, but the accommodation does no good if a student is not maintaining a routine that has them taking their medication on time in the morning and otherwise following a pattern of behavior that allows them to function during certain hours of the day. Having the capacity to maintain a routine of behavior is important to many students. What follows are the life skills that should be part of a student's routine before they are considered ready to make the transition to a STEM university.

Medication

Families share responsibilities amongst family members. In the families I work with, most often one person—yes, it is usually Mom—ends up responsible for making sure everyone else takes their medicine. In my own family, my mother sits down once a week with a bag full of pill bottles, a weekly pill organizer for both her and my father, and she makes sure they both have the medication they need to take at several times during the day correctly divided by day and time for the entire week. I have several medicines that I have to take once a day; Mom tried to set me up with a multi-compartmental pill box system that she could fill once a month for me. This system didn't work for me. I can literally look at this big white pillbox every day and not see it.

My memory is seriously weak in some areas. When it comes to medication I find there are two things that help me get my medicine on time and regularly: (1) routine, (2) visual reminders that work for me. The white pillbox does not work—seeing the actual pill containers on my kitchen counter first thing in the morning does work. Since there is no one in my home that I have to worry about taking my medicine, I have the ability to leave the bottles where I can see them on the counter. I then had to work on developing the routine of making sure taking my medicine was something I did in the morning. This was not an easy habit to develop and it took practice. Some mornings I forgot and then I suffered the side-effects of forgetting, which include a headache and nauseous feeling that lasts all afternoon. That sick feeling helped me remember that I needed to take my medication in the morning and I became more conscious of the need when I returned home and saw the pill bottles.

Caregivers need to realize that their young adults may need trial and error in order to learn the practice of taking medication but it is a vital practice that should be in place before they leave home to attend university. Remember, once in university they are considered adults and are expected to be responsible for their own medication, and no one will be standing there to remind them. Students need to have practiced being responsible for taking their own medication before they arrive on campus. This means they may have some bad days at home or in high school because they forgot their medicine but sooner or later they will have to live through the side-effects of not taking medicine on time—better that they do this at home as part of their learning, than in the higher-risk, higher-stress environment of a new university.

Creating a Medication Routine

When working on creating a routine that helps a student remember to take their own medication, it is important to remember the final context where this practice will be put into place, that is, the dorm room. The student cannot leave their medication sitting out in public view in a dorm room because dorm rooms will inevitably have some level of traffic other than the students who live there. As a result, medicine that is left out will disappear. Students may pick it up because they want to use it themselves and don't have a prescription, because it has "street value" and they can sell it, or because they are collecting prescriptions for a pharmaceutical party. A "pharm party" is when a group of people get together with all the prescription drugs they can get their hands on—parents', grandparents', siblings', their own—mix all these combined pills into one big bowl and then everyone takes a handful and hopes to get high. Practically speaking, whatever the reason, meds that are left out in the open will be taken.

Note to parents

Here is some advice for helping a student remember to take medicine in the context of living in a shared space:

- Have the student practice filling their own daily-reminder pill box once a week, on the same day at approximately the same time, for example Sunday evening while they watch a particular TV show, or Saturday evening before they sit down to play their favorite computer game.

- Encourage the student to keep the filled pill box in a drawer that they will look in every morning, for example their underwear or sock drawer.

- Encourage them to make a habit of picking the pill box up once in the morning and checking to see if the pill for that day has been taken.

I always recommend storing the majority of one's medicine in a locked box that is out of sight and only taking out a week's supply at a time. Teach students to handle their medicine in private, not in front of others. (When students are learning this practice it may be necessary to have "surprise inspections" during the week to check on their progress.) I also always advise students, *never discuss the medicine you take or its value with other students.* We have yet to have a student's room thoroughly searched to see if they have medicine worth stealing; we did have a case where a student made it public knowledge that he had a large quantity of valuable meds. He then kept the meds in an unlocked, top-desk drawer in a shared room. Someone opened the drawer, saw the medicine sitting there, and took it. One does not have to be a career criminal to pocket something of high value that is easily accessible. Sometimes people take things just because they can.

There are other ways of establishing medication routines and the advantage of starting to work on a routine before the student leaves home is that if what is first tried doesn't work, other systems can be tried.

- Consider posting a small desk calendar where it will be seen when the student wakes up—they have to put a sticker on the day when they take their meds, but cannot put the sticker on the day until after they have taken their meds.

- Use a page-a-day calendar and the student cannot remove the page until after taking their medicine.

- Encourage the student to use the reminder feature on their phone.

- If the student lives online, have them use an electronic calendar that flashes a reminder once a day, or sends them an instant message or email as a daily reminder.

No one method works equally well for all people. Thus it is preferable to start practicing taking one's own medicine by the time one is a senior in high school. That allows a year of trial, error, and establishment of a routine that will continue to work once a student is no longer at home.

Personal Hygiene

How often does a child still need reminding to take a shower, use deodorant, brush their teeth, or wash their hair? If a young person still has to be reminded of personal hygiene, then consider that this student is not yet prepared for the transition to university. Again, this is a pattern of behavior, a routine of self-care that needs to be practiced and mastered as a personal skill before a student leaves for university. Some students will not see the need for regular self-care. They may not realize that a lack of physical exertion does not stop personal body odor from building up on a person or on clothes that are worn repeatedly between washing. If a student is already sporadic in their personal hygiene, having to share a bathroom is likely to make them even more reluctant to follow a personal care routine.

Transitioning to shared bathroom spaces is difficult for most students—it is increasingly common for students to have never had to share a bedroom before arriving on campus; many will never have shared a bathroom with anyone but family members. Virtually every student would like a private room and a bath. Most campuses cannot accommodate this desire. On our campus, only a handful of students will be able to have private rooms with baths, no matter how much they are willing to pay. When it comes to a disabled students' waiting list for private baths, I sit down with the Director of Housing and we basically create a triage list based on need. Given all the information and documentation available to us, we decide who most needs the single baths and assign them in order of need. Someone who cannot physically maneuver in a standard washroom will be given priority for a handicapped washroom over someone with any other need. Those who are left will be divided between the remaining private washrooms, until we run out of spaces. So far, thanks in large part to the hard work of Housing, we've always managed to accommodate those with a legitimate need for a private washroom; we have not been able to accommodate everyone who would have preferred a private washroom.

Creating a Personal Hygiene Routine

All this is a reminder that if a student is not practiced in the routine of regular care for their personal hygiene, then the dorm room or shared apartment environment is only going to encourage further distancing from use of shared bathroom spaces. It is one of the least favorite responsibilities amongst Housing staff to have to take a young person aside and explain to him or her that they need to wash with soap regularly. Students are already anxious about being in a new space. Virtually everyone wants to feel that they are fitting in. Being prepared to maintain a personal hygiene routine that includes using soap, shampoo, and deodorant can go a long way towards helping a student fit into their new environment. Failure to maintain personal hygiene will almost always lead to the student standing out in a negative way to other students, staff, and faculty.

Note to Parents

- Discuss with the student why they are adapting a personal daily hygiene routine—there is a cultural and social expectation of personal care that they need to meet to be successful in college and in a career.

- Establish exactly what the elements of the daily personal hygiene routine will be: washing with soap, shampooing and later brushing hair, brushing teeth, applying deodorant.

- Encourage the student to automatically follow this routine each day.

- Encourage dressing in fresh, clean clothes each day as part of this routine.

Laundry

Laundry is another family chore that tends to fall to one or two people within the family. It may require an adjustment to the whole family's routine to teach a student how to sort, wash, dry, and fold their own clothes. Again, this is true for many students, not just invisibly disabled students. I was reminded of this one morning during an English Composition class I was teaching at a liberal arts university. While some professors arrive just as it is time to begin a class, I make a point of arriving so that I have at least five minutes to talk to students before class starts—as a result I not only learn a lot about what is happening in their lives but I also end up getting a number of general life questions. On one particular morning I could tell a young man had something he wanted to ask me but wasn't sure about. I looked him in the eye and nodded encouragingly. He responded by saying, "If I washed my laundry a week ago and put it in a laundry basket and then forgot about it, do I have to wash it again before I wear it, or if it's dried can I wear it anyway?"

The OCD part of me internally grimaced at the thought of moldy laundry. I matter of factly responded, "Yep. You need to wash that again." He nodded, less interested in a learning moment than in having a sneaking suspicion confirmed…even if it did require a little more effort on his part to re-wash his clothes.

Students generally want to meet social expectations that will allow them to fit in with their peers. They require someone to teach them what these social expectations are and how to meet them, particularly if their disability keeps them from being able to easily realize what prevailing social expectations are. Routines and patterns are very useful for helping students with invisible disabilities carry out daily tasks in new environments and during times of stress. Waiting until a few weeks before a student leaves home to teach them how to do their laundry, or when and why they need to clean their own clothes is not sufficient time for this to become an established routine.

Creating a Laundry Routine

A colleague in Housing shared this story with me. One day when he was making the rounds of the laundry area in his building he came across a student who was placing a single pair of white socks into the washing machine.

"What are you doing?"

The student's response, "My mother told me to wash my whites separately."

This story may or may not be an urban legend. The point is, when students are told how to do something without being given the opportunity for mentored, hands-on experience, they will not learn as well. Teaching the routine of how laundry is done means showing and explaining, then allowing the student to practice, with ample time allowed for a student's need to continue practicing until she has established a new routine.

When I was in college one of my friends had 30 identical pairs of white underwear. When her underwear drawer was almost empty, she knew she had to make time to do laundry. She had a sufficient supply of other clothes that she could find clean things to wear until her underwear supply was almost used up—then she spent a day doing her mounds of laundry. For most people though, I recommend that laundry become a weekly habit so that when it is time to do laundry the amount of clothes to be washed is not overwhelming.

The cost of doing laundry in dormitory buildings is usually low or free. Currently students in our dorm halls can wash their laundry for free, and dry a load for 25 cents. I did have a student who lives off campus, with an extensive wardrobe, tell me, however, that when she went to a local laundry-mat to wash and dry clothes it cost her $50—an argument to my mind for either staying on campus or limiting one's laundry to clothes that can be washed in two or three loads once a week. If personal style does not allow a student to limit their laundry needs to a few loads a week, then one should make doing laundry a budget criterion that is accounted for each semester. This is another reason why having an established laundry routine before leaving for university is useful—it allows the student to realize how much time and money they need to set aside each week for keeping up with laundry.

Some students choose to do laundry twice a month, or every two weeks. How realistic this is depends on the limits of the student's wardrobe and their willingness to spend a longer amount of time doing laundry. Two weeks' worth of clothes will take more loads— three or four—and will take longer to dry and fold. Students also need to understand that wearing the same clothes repeatedly during the two-week stretch is not socially acceptable, particularly once the clothes start to appear dirty, or start to hold food and body odors. With many students being very sensitive to smell, including other invisibly disabled students, a lack of a sense of personal smell should not lead a student to believe he can forgo doing laundry.

Most faculty and staff are also sensitive to the smell of unwashed bodies and laundry, and just like future employers and co-workers in a work environment, they will not want to spend time with a student who has what is found to be an objectionable odor. Students need to practice the personal hygiene skills that will allow them to hold a job and work with and around others. Intelligence is not the only factor that is considered when hiring someone who will be working closely with co-workers. No one wants to spend their days in an office, laboratory, or vehicle with a colleague who ignores their personal hygiene.

Note to Students
Doing laundry

With the color array of most student wardrobes being limited, laundry can often be divided into three loads, washed once a week:

- Place used pants/jeans/shorts/dark socks in one pile.

- Place used shirts/underwear/light socks in another pile.

- Place used towels, face cloths, sheets in a pile.

- Wash each pile as a separate load in cold water, with laundry soap.

- Dry and fold or hang up shirts and pants immediately after washing.

- Dry, fold, and put back in dresser the socks and underwear.

- Dry sheets and towels—put the sheets back on the bed, and either fold and store the towels, or hang them back up.

- Pay attention to the load limit on a washing machine. If the machine is overloaded it can overflow with water and soap—the person responsible for overloading the machine can be held responsible for the cost of repairing the machine if that should be necessary.

I can say that as I am out and about on campus I daily encounter students who have not been convinced of the need for personal hygiene. Unwashed clothes, unwashed people can make meetings in a small space a real challenge. I can think of several students who are notable because every time they come into my office *they smell clean…* not cologned or perfumed, just clean. For people who intend to become professionals, learning to maintain a neutral or non-offensive odor is an important skill that should be acquired before they come to university—this leaves one less thing for the student to attempt to learn once they are in university; if the skill isn't learned by the time they arrive on campus it is often hard for the student to adapt to this expectation.

Meal Preparation

The majority of freshmen students will live in dormitories for their first year on a STEM campus. Community colleges are most likely to have students who live off campus. Beyond the first year, many students will find themselves living in housing where they are responsible for their own cooking. Even in a dormitory, students will usually have access to a shared kitchen on a floor in their dorm; many students have microwaves and small refrigerators in their rooms. Yet, a large number of students have little or no experience of cooking.

I am in agreement with the thinking that every person should have one or two "emergency dishes" they can prepare in a kitchen: pasta, rice, meat correctly cooked without a barbeque—something that requires more than heating a pre-packaged meal in the microwave or adding hot water. From a practical point of view, pre-packaged meals are usually the most expensive and least nutrient-rich choice available, with less fiber, more salt and sugar than a "homemade" equivalent would contain, even when some of the homemade ingredients come from other packages. And it can be incredibly frustrating to be hungry and have a microwave breakdown, leaving a person unable to cook something with a stove top or oven that is still available.

Creating a Meal Preparation Routine

Within the last year an alumni magazine I was reading featured a full-page story about a former student who had made a huge impact on his dorm hall-mates. Using a hot plate, one frying pan, and a couple of bowls, this student created small hotcakes using a pre-packaged flour mix and water; topped the hotcakes with fresh sliced strawberries and whipped cream, and served them from his dorm room. He didn't start out to serve his whole hall but word quickly spread and he soon had the most popular room on the floor. Over two decades later fellow students who had partaken in that makeshift meal were still talking about it.

Hot plates are banned in dorm rooms now, but shared kitchens are often available at a centralized location in each hall or dorm building. With most students relying on dorm food for subsistence, something like a "homemade" hotcake with fresh fruit is an understandably welcome chance to share and hang out with other students. If there are one or two meals a student can make, this can create an opportunity to share something with friends; also, practicing cooking so that one is better prepared for life as an adult will make that part of the transition easier in the long run too.

Note to parents

Families should work together to create a practice of meal preparation:

- Allow children to cook/bake in the kitchen with adults—cooking is best learned hands on.

- Plan for one meal a week that is cooked with children.

- As children learn and grow, have them prepare one main dish a week.

- By the senior year of high school, work with the student on meal planning and shopping so that they can prepare one entire meal at least once a month, including knowing how to shop for the necessary ingredients.

If your family has a student who is on the verge of leaving for college and who has no real cooking experience, then go back to basics. Focus on assisting the student with learning a few easy-to-cook dishes that don't require a lot of preparation—or dishes:

- Pasta with a heated sauce—needs one pot, one pan.

- Eggs that are scrambled or an omelet with pre-shredded cheese—needs a bowl and a pan.

- Rice in a rice steamer with fried vegetables and/or meat—needs a rice steamer and a pan.

- Meat that is baked in the oven (the student needs to know the oven temperature and the cooking time) with carrots, sweet potatoes, squash, or other ingredients which can be added during baking, for a one-dish meal—needs only a baking dish.

A meal does not need to be complicated to provide a welcome break from dorm food, or to help stretch a budget instead of constantly buying take-out. Students who have difficulty focusing or who are prone to stress, however, will benefit greatly from the opportunity to have had practice making a meal enough times to feel comfortable doing so. They will also benefit from practice focusing on the task at hand before they're in a dorm hall, setting off smoke alarms because they didn't realize what would happen if they wandered out of the community kitchen and forgot about what they were cooking...yes, I've had to deal with students who have done this more than once, and in one case a student who was asked to leave her housing as a result of her tendency to set dishes on fire due to her lack of attention to what she was doing.

In families where cooking is something that no one has traditionally practiced, it certainly is possible for family members to learn together. Cook books of simple meals are available, cooking classes for those learning to cook are offered in many communities, and if a family can approach cooking with a sense of fun and adventure, then trial and error can be a great way to learn. By learning some of the basics of cooking at home, a student is better prepared for the transition into adulthood and independent life. They also have one more skill they can use to draw positive attention from peers.

Transportation

Not all students are interested in being drivers. Amongst those who are interested in driving, there are complications to having a car on campus as a first-year student. Freshmen are often required to park far from where they live, if they are allowed to have a car on the main campus at all. Car insurance can be cost prohibitive, as is the cost of maintaining another family vehicle. If the student herself is responsible for making car or insurance payments, then the need to work can get in the way of studying. And in particularly inclement weather not only are car accidents more likely but trudging to and from the car to the dorm room can be a great disadvantage in getting out and doing necessary chores like going to a doctor or picking up medication.

In other words, students should be capable of taking a bus. For a handful of families this may sound like redundant advice, as their students have been taking city buses for years before leaving for college. Such students are in the minority amongst all the students I have met. Many students have either received transportation from their family, particularly their parents, or they have driven themselves places. I recently had a young man in my office who was feeling particularly stressed because for the first time as a young driving adult he could not look out of his window and see his truck parked waiting for him. Separation anxiety from easily available transportation is real; I've witnessed it many times. Physically practicing how to discover where a city's bus route is, what it is like to take a bus, how to have one's money prepared—these practical skills can reduce the stress of using transportation in a new town where a student will already have a number of other anxiety issues to deal with. Every year I deal with students who have never taken a bus, do not know where to catch a bus and have no practical experience with discovering information about bus schedules, costs, and routes.

Creating a Transportation Routine

By the senior year of high school, a student should be learning how to get to several specific locations without the assistance of parents driving them. This does not mean that parents or other family members completely stop driving them to places; I am suggesting that they have regular practice with getting to their destinations without being driven by family. This also means not being reliant on friends to drive them. If a family budget can afford for a student to travel for four or five years by taxi, then parents can work with a student on how to make arrangements for a cab when they need to go to the doctor, or to the pharmacy to pick up medicine. Otherwise, parents are advised to take a bus several times with their student, then have them take the bus sometimes by themselves. This may prove to be a learning experience for the entire family.

Note to Parents

- Check online for the bus schedule.

- Make certain that the student is prepared with the correct money to travel both directions of their trip.

- Make certain that the student knows how to determine the correct time and place to catch a bus—nothing will reinforce stress like waiting in the wrong place, or at the wrong time.

- Once you have traveled a route with your student, make sure he uses the route on his own.

- Assist the student in learning more than one route, since they will need the ability to be adaptable to a new route at university.

- If the student will need to use an elevated train or subway instead of a bus, allow enough time with them in their new environment to practice taking the new route, on the new mode of transportation, with them.

Anxiety and stress over the unknown and unexperienced is probably the most common experience shared by nearly everyone with an invisible disability. Making the time to practice and experience new events with your invisibly disabled student can prepare them to discover and experience new things once they are on their own. Discuss their fears with them and talk them through, "What's the worst thing that can happen?"

For example, the "worst thing that can happen" related to travel is usually the fear of getting lost and ending up in a strange place, and not being certain how to get back to familiar territory. It can be helpful to talk through what can be done in such a circumstance.

Note to Parents

- Discuss that transportation lines work in both directions; if one traveled by public transport from point A to point B, then public transport goes in the opposite direction from point B to point A. Assist a student in learning how to get back from where they end up.

- There can be an underlying fear of strangers; remind students that they have a cell phone which they can use, that if a crime is taking place they can call the police, that if they need to talk to someone they can call family, or a crisis line. Make sure they have the correct phone numbers for these calls programmed into their phone.

- Sometimes fear is of the unknown; making time to use public transport in the new environment with a student can remove some of this fear.

Shopping

I have worked with one young man who on at least two different occasions has asked me how to buy what I would consider basic necessities. Once he wanted aspirin, once he wanted deodorant. He had a general idea that he could find both these items in a large pharmacy store; we have no large pharmacy stores in town. What was he to do?

For those with more life experience, particularly those who shop for an entire family, it may seem that some advice is so obvious that it does not need teaching. Learning to shop is a complex social activity, however; remember there was once a President of the US who upon re-entering a grocery store for the first time in decades was amazed to see a bar-code scanner and was unfamiliar with the technology. If you do not shop, you do not know how shopping works—presidents are not the only ones who have others do shopping for them. Some students arrive at college never having grocery shopped and having had their clothes purchased by another family member for them.

Creating a Shopping Routine

Some families look for the best economical bargain when shopping. Others have certain brand names they trust. And food shopping is often an extension of cooking, that is to say the flavor of some familiar dishes may depend on using certain types of ingredients. I have a cousin who was frustrated when a family member asked for her recipe for spinach dip and then complained that the spinach dip did not taste the same: "Did you hold out on some of the ingredients?" Further questioning revealed, however, that the new cook had substituted other ingredients for the mayonnaise and sour cream the recipe called for. If you buy different ingredients and put them into a recipe, you will get a different taste. Family culture influences how we shop, how we cook, and what makes a purchase a relative "bargain."

Note to Parents

- If a student finds shopping unpleasant, then keep store trips to the basics—personal hygiene and food—and help them discover the world of online shopping for other needs.

- Explain what you are looking for when you seek out an ingredient or item. Do you value price, name brand, sales, coupons; there is no one way to shop but everyone needs a place to start.

- Take time when bringing a student to campus to help them discover where local stores are and identify how they can get to the store; for many invisibly disabled students, making a trip to the store with them can reduce anxiety about being in a new place to shop.

I personally do not enjoy shopping—most of the time. I learned methods for shopping by accompanying different family members to the store. Clothes shopping with my maternal grandmother— for woolen winter clothes in summer—was torture; grocery shopping with my mother was bearable because she made a list and methodically worked through the store getting what our family needed. As a dyslexic person I usually find the best way to shop is to walk through sections of a store and recall by sight when I am in need of something. As someone who doesn't like crowds, I prefer to do this in smaller stores where I'm not overwhelmed by quantities of different types of things, or a lot of people. I avoid large chain stores in favor of smaller, local stores. I probably pay slightly more for goods than those who only shop in large chain stores, however, the bargain for me is in the peace of mind avoiding such stores gives me.

One of the things the research from my doctorate degree showed was the best way for a person to learn how to do something was to learn side by side from someone with more experience, followed by opportunities to practice the new knowledge or skill, and to gradually work their way towards becoming independent with that knowledge and the abilities they learned. I am not the first person to make this observation, my research simply proved that this way of learning carries over into an even wider array of knowledge than people usually realize, including using reading and writing.

What my own disabilities, life experience, and work have shown me is that this kind of learning—through opportunities to practice and develop routines—carries over into practices like taking medicine, shopping, making appointments, personal hygiene habits, cooking, and doing laundry. Any student should be able to do these things before they are considered ready to attend college. This knowledge is vital for invisibly disabled students for the following reasons:

- They are more likely to experience anxiety related to new people and situations.

- They are more likely to be overwhelmed and shut down by anxiety.

- They are less likely to be able to problem-solve without support.

- They will be removed from their normal support network when away from home.

- They are more likely to be some distance from home in a STEM university.

Making sure these are all practices that an invisibly disabled student has experience and routines to deal with, increases the likelihood that the student will be successful in her transition from home to a new school.

These life skills are just part of what a student needs to know. These are the practices and knowledge that a student best learns at home. Some of what a student needs practice with will also come from practices that combine home and school life; these are the practices that will next be discussed. Once a family, including their STEM-bound student, begin to understand the difference in context that is being prepared for, it will begin to be clearer why some of the hard-fought-for accommodations at school might require phasing out by the time the student graduates from high school. As these changes are discussed it will also help clarify if a student is immediately ready for the transition to a STEM university, or if they would be better served by first attending a local community college or regional university.

3

What Students Need to Know Before Class Starts

The mother was matter of fact, not realizing that what she was about to ask me was completely out of step with how our competitive STEM university operates. "Will we be meeting the aide that the university provides our son, or will you choose that person without us?" Her student had used the accommodation of a personal aide throughout high school. While he was incredibly intelligent, he did not do well with social situations, had not been active in his own note-taking, and his high school had basically excused him from all group work. This was a young man who was not prepared to be at a STEM school in any way except for his specialized knowledge in math and science. The preparation he lacked would prove to be his undoing in university.

While this student was able to otherwise function, he had never been responsible for getting through a class day on his own. His aide had facilitated his functioning within his high school; he was used to having an adult assist him with day-to-day classroom behavior and details. It emotionally pains me that such intelligent young people are not prepared for university, or university for them. The lack of preparation to function independently became apparent as he soon showed his inability to get through classes now that his aide was no longer there to monitor his behavior. I will come back to this young man's story in Chapter 5. At this point I use him as an example of what to my mind is a troubling question: When does a school aide stop aiding a student? This is a complex question with a complicated answer.

An Appropriate Level of Aid

I understand only too well the need for aids for some students. Some people are very intelligent but lack the ability to socially function. It needs to be pointed out, however, that a person's ability to function socially can to some degree be learned through repeated practice. I regularly work with young people who while not born with the ability to pick up social cues and expectations by observation, have been taught the rules of social expectations in certain contexts. There was one young man I remember precisely because it was so clear that he had been taught, and had been required to practice, social conventions that had no meaning to him but that he recognized as "expected." He was uncomfortable with eye contact or social pleasantries but diligently worked at carrying out the social rules he had been taught. One day I saw him sitting in the waiting area of my office. I walked over to say hello and he responded by lowering his gaze to the floor next to me and—from his seated position—raised his hand, shook my hand and said, "Good afternoon, how are you today?" I became very fond of this young man and his earnest effort to find a place in the world which would allow him to put his intelligence to work. The fact that his family appeared to have put great effort into helping him memorize the correct social behavior for different contexts, and that he in turn tried to faithfully carry it out, showed the work he was prepared to do in order to have a place in society.

I do not wish to be a proponent of the attitude that people who are socially uncomfortable must always make great efforts to 'fit in.' Rather, I have seen over and over that the difference between young people who become socially successful and are able to work, and those who will spend their lives in group homes or remain with their family, often has more to do with the dedication a family and educators show to helping a student meet a degree of social expectations than it has to do with a child's intelligence. I have met several families with students who were born with Down's syndrome, who worked hard with their children so that the child would realize their fullest potential; these children went on to hold jobs in local businesses, such as cleaning in a bakery. I worked with another boy with Down's syndrome whose family decided their only intervention would be to pray for a miracle. This child was not able to perform basic self-care tasks, despite intense intervention by specialists in his school district. While he was capable of much more, his family would do nothing to work with him; they would not even teach him to dress himself. By the time I encountered him at a special needs summer camp, he was ten, morbidly obese, and needed an aid for everything, including using the bathroom.

I use children with Down's syndrome as an example to show that people born with similar disabilities can have very different outcomes based on the role a family chooses to play in their child's life, and based on what the family considers to be realistic expectations...not impossible expectations, but realistic. In my current work I encounter students with disabilities that similarly impact their potential but who, due to different socialization and education in-home from their family, along with support from their school, display very different outcomes. Which brings me back to my original question—what is an appropriate level of aid?

As I established in Chapter 2, my studies and others have shown that we best learn how to do new-to-us activities when we have the opportunity for learning from someone who already has the know-how, and then are able to put our new knowledge into practice. Any child needs to learn what the social expectations in their family and larger group are; some children will learn this largely through observations, other children will require more explicit teaching. The fact that a child is socially awkward, has anxiety disorder, or needs very explicit instruction is not in my mind an excuse for not providing this education. Similarly, if a child has the intelligence and potential for eventually attending a STEM university, then there should be instruction given that allows this child to know what classroom expectations are, and practice to meet the expectation of an average classroom.

The appropriate "necessary level of aid" then means that a child is prevented from harming themselves or others, but not that they are excused from learning how to participate in class, hand in assignments on time, or sit in a classroom without disturbing the rest of the class. This is not to suggest that a child be forced into carrying out activities that are physically or emotionally beyond their capacity but that the limits of their capacity are slowly increased through trial and routine. If a student's goal is to attend a STEM university, then they must be able to self-regulate their behavior, manage their own stress with the aid of a counselor or medication, arrive at class on time without supervision, prepare for class having obtained the correct textbooks, and arrange for academic support such as a note-taker if their disability interferes with note-taking. The student must be able to actively participate in their own education without an aide being responsible for them.

In a crowded high school classroom, as an increasing number of classes are, it may seem impossible to teach if one has a student whose behavior is disruptive. This is why support from parents at home is so important—schools and families must work together to best educate a student. A student who learns at home that there are times when they are expected to sit and either talk in a reasonable tone of voice to others, or listen, will have skills to bring to school and further there. For example, a family that sits down at dinner together, takes turns talking about their day, and learns to listen when others are sharing—has also better prepared their student to start practice sitting and listening for 20–30 minute stretches at school. These habits take time and practice, and the ability to focus on or participate in such activities increases over time. I would not expect any young child to be able to quietly sit still for an hour at a time; even teaching at a university level I do not expect to keep a student's attention for more than 15–20 minutes before I will switch activities from large group to small group work or otherwise alter the pace of what is happening. How a student can respond in a college environment, though, is based on what they have learned in their previous education. If a student has only been able to sit quietly in a classroom because an adult was sitting next to them, I do not expect them to be ready for classrooms beyond high school.

Finding Textbooks

Before a student arrives at university, textbooks have almost exclusively been given to them in a classroom setting. It really isn't surprising then, that most students arrive on university campuses not sure where and how to get text books. When a student is living with an invisible disability, it is very likely that they also live with a level of elevated stress. Anxiety seems to accompany invisible disabilities rather like rain clouds tend to accompany rain; a lack of clouds on a rainy day is an exception, not the rule. Added to the anxiety of transitioning to a new living arrangement, new geography, new food, new people... trying to find textbooks can be the straw that breaks a student's back. At least once a semester I will meet with a student who has either not bought any of his textbooks a month into the first semester, or who has only purchased some of his textbooks—not due to a lack of money but due to being overwhelmed by the process.

Correcting this situation is not as simple as pointing a student in the direction of the campus bookstore. In fact, to successfully find the correct book for a class, a student needs to start this process with extracting more details from their class registration information. Every course has a course number and section number. A student needs both those numbers to make sure the textbook(s) she buys for each class are correct for the section of the class she has signed up for. The name of the professor may change but if a student has the correct course and section number, then she will be able to find the correct text—if necessary by asking for assistance from the staff of the bookstore.

Not all students are best served by purchasing a standard textbook (or renting, which is becoming a more popular option). There are at least two online options for buying or renting e-textbooks; these e-textbooks provide access to both the written text and an electronic version of the textbook that can be listened to. At the time of writing, in the US, Bookshare is a source of e-textbooks that is being funded by the US Department of Education Office of Special Education Programs (OSEP) and is able to provide free e-textbooks to qualified individuals (students with visual and reading disabilities). Unfortunately for STEM students, many of the textbooks that are required are not available through Bookshare. We have found the majority of our texts available through CourseSmart. CourseSmart makes e-textbooks available on a rental basis for different periods of time, since schools have semesters of different lengths. The advantages of CourseSmart texts are not just that they are e-textbooks which can be listened to as well as read; a student with a computer and a textbook's ISBN number (or title, current edition number, and authors) can order a text from their home computer, completely avoiding the crowds and stress of a bookstore at the beginning of a semester.[1]

Another advantage of CourseSmart and Bookshare is that they allow access to both the aural e-text and the written text by way of a person's computer—a student can print out pages to take to class with them, not just listen to the textbook. This is particularly handy for STEM students because some textbooks will include graphs, mathematical formulas, or other visual information that a student will need to see—something which an e-text alone does not offer. With the increasing demand for e-text, more publishers are also moving to offering textbooks electronically; students with greater computer proficiency are starting to order e-texts directly from publishers.

Note-Taking Supplies and Technology

Another recurring challenge amongst students with invisible disabilities is maintaining organization. By the time a student is ready to leave for college, he should have worked towards a system for keeping information from different classes separate and identifiable. For some students separate notebooks of different colors work; some students prefer a single notebook with dividers or even a binder with divisions. Generally I am in favor of staying with a system that has already proven successful—which means developing a successful system before the student graduates from high school. That said, a large binder for everything will be a disadvantage in college. Students on our campus, for example, may have to walk between three or four different buildings during their freshman year, without access to a locker to switch books. That means the student will be carrying books and notebooks around with him and one bulky binder for everything means hauling all of one's notes and handouts everywhere. Since not all classes meet every day, a student can at least leave the notes and books they don't need on a particular day in their dorm room. This brings up another point in favor of e-texts; the student only has to print out the text-pages they will be using on a particular day to bring to class, reducing some of the strain on their backs and shoulders from carrying large science and math texts. If a student's disabilities include fibromyalgia or impaired mobility, then reducing

---

1   Another advantage of online book sources is that they are available globally, provided one has computer access. Bookshare: www.bookshare.org. CourseSmart: www.coursesmart.com.

their backpack load to a few notebooks and some printed pages of text can make a big difference in their overall health and feeling of wellbeing.

A number of invisible disabilities complicate the process of note-taking. As a dyslexic person, for example, I must focus on what a professor says one minute, write that down as quickly as possible—missing what the professor says while I write—and then listen to the next bit of information when I'm done writing. This means on a good day I'm focusing on half of what is said in class. My other option is to focus on everything that is said and write down basically no notes until after class. I've talked to people with AD/HD, reading and learning disabilities who find they are in the same predicament—listen or write. There are at least two possible solutions to this dilemma.

Note-taker

For those with a qualifying disability that keeps them from being able to listen and take their own notes, schools typically provide the accommodation of a note-taker in class. This may be a paid or volunteer position but the purpose is to provide the disabled student with a set of clear notes that someone else has taken during the class. This does not mean a student can skip class and still obtain the notes; schools will only hand on the notes taken if the student attends class. In order to obtain a note-taker a student must first identify herself to the student disability service provider on campus. These offices have different names and may be found in the Student Service Center on a campus. If a student is having trouble locating the office responsible for disability services, then the Dean of Students or Chancellor's office will be able to offer direction to the correct person to contact. Every campus has someone responsible for ensuring disabled students have the support necessary as mandated by the law.

Technology

Some students prefer to take their own notes because this allows them to begin processing the information as they are listening to what the professor says and they write. They may still have concerns about missing some information or not fully processing what is being said. For these students recording a professor with a digital recorder has proven useful. Currently in such cases I favor a technology that allows for the recording and note-taking to work together.

The Livescribe company has developed what was originally marketed as the Pulse Pen, revised and currently marketed as the Echo™ Smartpen. The Echo™ is an oversized pen. The larger than average pen size is due to an internal microchip which records both the audio and writing during a class, so the pen captures what the student writes on the Livescribe paper and the sound of the professor's voice (and some ambient background noise, so don't eat a bag of chips while trying to use it, as one student I know did). This pen is showing up increasingly in meetings as people in general find it useful to be able to go back to places in their notes and be reminded of the discussion surrounding different points they had written down. The pen needs to be used with microdot paper the company also produces. The pen recharges through a docking station that connects to a computer. This is also how notes—both written and voice—can be downloaded to a computer.

Reading Handouts

Sometimes as part of taking notes a student will find it necessary to read and possibly respond to handouts. There are technologies available now that allow a student to magnify written words or that will read to students. These can be useful for some reading disabilities, some forms of dyslexia, and for students who have difficulty tracking words with both eyes at once. Unlike the Livescribe company which currently holds the patent on advanced recording pens that store written and oral communication, there are more choices for how to magnify pre-printed text. The disability service provider on a campus can also arrange for a student to be provided with handouts that are in a larger font or meet other needs, such as more white space on the page or between words. To prepare for the discussion with the disability service provider a student should be conscious of how their disability affects their ability to process written words, and have some ideas about what works for them, such as larger print, white space, etc.

Service Providers

Colleges have several types of service providers who can be very important to the invisibly disabled student's academic success, while others provide services that can improve the quality of life experience a student has. Students will also have opportunities to join student activity and sports groups, fraternities/sororities, honor societies, intermural leagues, and arrange to volunteer for social groups like Big Sisters or the Society for the Prevention of Cruelty to Animals (SPCA).[2] There are students on our campus who do all of these; sometimes an academic counselor or service provider will need to talk to a student about not being so active in social groups. While there is a great deal of choice available for students on every college campus, no one will force students to take part in these opportunities and no one will force them to leave a group. If a group behaves in a manner that is prohibited by a school's conduct policy the group may be banned from the school but no one will keep the students from talking to each other. Again, a student who arrives on campus unable to seek out service or manage their own time is not necessarily going to be on campus long enough to learn these skills. Chapter 6 will further discuss the importance of social networking for both personal and professional development.

Student Disability Services

One more thing that changes from high school to college is the school's responsibility to seek out disabled students. Once a student enters college the responsibility lies with the student and his family to seek out the service provider. If after checking a school's website it is not clear who the disability service provider is, contact the Dean of Students' office for this information. The Dean of Students' office or Chancellor's office is also a good contact for students who have questions that they do not know how to find answers to; this office is also responsible for generating the honors list of students each semester—the listing for students who maintain high grades;

---

2   In the US and Canada there are different kinds of student organizations which run independently of the university and have national/international associations. These can be fraternal organizations with a range of service and professional goals (fraternities for males, sororities for females), or grade/field of study based (honor societies, usually open to all genders). Big Sisters/Big Brothers are volunteer service organizations that provide mentors for girls and boys.

they work with students identifying sources for academic support; if a student should have to leave school during a semester or have a significant life-event then it is preferable to inform the Dean/ Chancellor so that the school as an entity is aware and can make sure the student has followed all necessary steps to leave the school in good standing and thus return in the future or transfer to another school.

In order for a student to receive accommodations in class— extended test time, large print handouts, a non-distracting test environment—the disability service provider will probably want to see documentation of the student's disability. What counts as documentation will vary from school to school. Some schools will look at an Individual Education Plan (IEP); others want to see a doctor's report of how the student's diagnosis was arrived at. The kind of documentation a school requires can usually be found on a school's website and again, when in doubt, the Dean or Chancellor's office can point a family in a clearer direction.

Academic Support Services

Learning centers have become a prominent feature of campus life. Historically the first learning centers to be present on a campus were usually for writing or math. As the importance of academic support becomes clearer, however, an increasing number of campuses are offering academic support for an increasing number of classes. On our campus basically every department has a learning center that supports the classes being taught by that department. Some schools house all their learning centers in one centralized location. Again, searching a school's website can tell a great deal about the kinds of services that are offered and where the different service providers are located. Increasingly campuses are moving towards something like a Student Support Service Center; what is available in such a center may not include all the academic supports actually available for students on that campus, so do not hesitate to ask questions regarding any further services that might be available.

Schools may also offer programs that are available to invisibly disabled students for an additional fee. These services usually include increased one-on-one academic counseling and tutoring. Several universities also train students who will accompany the invisibly disabled student to class and assist with notes and study. This is as close to having a personal aide as a university environment currently allows and the money to pay the student-assistant usually comes from the family or insurance; this kind of expense is considered personal and will not be covered by the school.

Counseling Services

Stress and depression have always been a part of student life. With the increasing awareness of invisibly disabled students on campus, including more awareness of mental health disabilities, most campuses now offer free or more affordable counseling services on campus. At the three public universities where I have taught, free counseling is available to any registered student. This is a service where demand by the end of the semester starts to overtake supply and waiting too long to make an appointment can mean waiting weeks to get in and see someone. If a student has a history of anxiety, depression, or difficulty avoiding "melt-downs" then it is wise to schedule an appointment with the campus counseling services at the beginning of the semester and maintain semi-regular appointments throughout the semester. It is easier to get on a counselor's schedule at the beginning of the semester than it will be once classes have been underway for a while.

A student who has benefited from counseling in the past should expect to use counseling services as part of their transition to college. This is a much more stressful transition than freshmen are ever ready for. Students tend to focus on the exciting aspects of being more independent and not having parents telling them as regularly what they have to do, what they have to eat, and when they can come and go. Even when nervous about the change it is difficult for a student to be prepared for how challenging a number of sometimes smaller changes at once can be. They no longer have constant access to prepared food or food they necessarily are accustomed to, they don't have their own bedroom to retreat to, their own TV with remote, and they may or may not get along with their dorm-mates. Then there are the more challenging classes, new professors, learning to read syllabi, being responsible for even more homework, and having to be responsible for their own choices about when to go out and when to focus on their work. To top this off, they cannot go home and complain to their family about the injustices and injuries to pride they may have had to suffer on any given day. University is exciting but invariably the transition creates stress.

The Good News

At this point family members may be looking at each other and wondering if their child should ever be "sent away" to school. If the student is intelligent, capable of functioning on his own, and able to live away from home then the answer is a resounding YES.

Here's the good news:

- At STEM university a student will encounter for perhaps the first time in his life people who can intelligently discuss the details of specialized interests that no one else has ever shared with him.

- He will find peers who share interests in the same kind of reading/role-playing/ popular culture/computer literacy, etc. that he has.

- He will meet professors who have been successful while living with the same kind of disabilities he lives with.

- He may find himself intellectually challenged for the first time in his life.

- He will find a culture that embraces his unique characteristics and people who pride themselves on being "different" from "everyone else."

- He will have hands-on opportunities to make, discover, work with the very kind of things that excite him.

STEM education is not for everyone. For those drawn to the fields of science, technology, engineering, and math, however, having the opportunity to spend time in an environment with like-minded people is something to be anticipated. It is a goal that is worth the time and effort that is required by student and family to be adequately prepared.

4

Successful Study

The young woman sitting across my desk from me set her large kinesiology textbook down with a thump, pages open to the chapter she was expected to read. I asked her, "What do you look at first when you read a chapter?"

"Uh, everything. I just read everything and that takes too long and...I don't know what to do." Her shoulders hunched in, she was the picture of frustration and defeat.

I regularly encounter young people who due to their intelligence have never really had to study before entering a highly competitive STEM school. In fact, some are able to get through the first year of their STEM education by floundering their way through texts and notes, relying on their ability to remember important chunks of what a professor said in class. Sooner or later though, they seem to hit the same wall this young woman had hit. They are no longer able to make good grades without having some idea what their textbooks say and they do not know how to efficiently get this information because it is a skill they've never had to make use of before. Studying is one more thing we assume people learn as they go through their high school education but not everyone does. High-functioning, invisibly disabled students are particularly likely to have relied on their intelligence and other skills—like a good memory for what is said by the teacher—and other techniques that allowed them to adapt to earlier knowledge. Their previous skill set cannot keep pace at a demanding university and for perhaps the first time ever they need to learn how to study.

I've found over the years as a disabled student, a teacher, and a disability service provider that there are better ways of getting information from textbooks than just spending more time reading them. There are ways of reading textbooks, what I call "insider information," that can be useful to struggling, intelligent students. I call this insider information because until someone teaches a student how to read a textbook, this useful information is like a secret that only those who have already learned it know. Human beings are not born knowing how to use books—we learn this from other humans when they take the time to explain how they use books, or by observing how others use books and then trying to mimic them. It is worth noting that not everyone uses books to learn and thus not all students will have had opportunities to observe family members using books to learn.

How to Read a Textbook

As a writer and teacher I value an ideal world where students carefully read their textbooks and have a deeper understanding of the topic being explained and taught within its pages. As a dyslexic student who studied philosophy and theology and the copious amounts of reading that went with these, I can testify that the ideal world doesn't exist for most students. Learning to do a combination of skim-reading and then stopping to pull out the "important details" in a text is an ability that has great use in university. For classroom purposes, an important detail is one that a professor values and will also be likely to test on.

Reading a book has to be done in a way that works with a student's disabilities and learning style. Some students can study late into the night; I quickly found out I was not one of those students. After attempting a few all-nighters I was forced to realize that my ability to read and process written words stops working after a certain point in the day. I learned that to be a successful student I needed to study earlier in the day while my brain was still able to make meaning from words. It is vital for the success of a student that he realizes how his own brain best functions given the combination of his disability, medication, sleep pattern, and learning style. If one's disability or medication limits the hours that one can productively study, then one either chooses to use their "good" study hours for study or increases the likelihood of being unsuccessful in class.

Table of Contents and Index

Reading a book is like being a detective; if one pays attention one will find clues that help solve the mystery of what each specific section of the book is meant to be teaching. A good way to learn more about the key ideas inside a book is to take time to read the Table of Contents. The Table of Contents shows how the textbook is going to break the ideas inside into units—or "chunks"—of information. The list of words and ideas there might seem initially intimidating but they will provide the reader with initial clues. Begin by reading the chapter title. Stop and think about the words—the title is a reader's first clue about what the chapter is meant to contain. Then look at the sub-section headings. They provide further clues that tell the reader where specific ideas will be explained within that chapter. If a professor has mentioned a particular topic in class several times and one of the sub-headings in a chapter has this topic in the title, then that is a section of the book where the reader can find more information or gain further understanding of what the professor is talking about. Another way to find more information about a topic that is being discussed in class is to look at the end of the book—in the Index.

A Table of Contents tells the reader how the book's main ideas will be laid out in the text. An Index tells the reader where to find more information about particular topics within the text. The Index alphabetically lists key words by the page numbers where that word or idea will be discussed or explained. When looking for a quick reminder about a particular topic or idea, look in the Index for places in the book that will provide this information. Looking in the Index of this book and looking up the word "Index," the page numbers listed would include this page. Between the Table of Contents and the Index, a reader will know where every main idea in the book can be found. I find it interesting that many students arrive at university not having been taught this. This is an important bit of insider information that students who need to use books can use to their benefit.

Reading a Chapter

A professor assigns a particular set of pages or chapter to read because the information in the chapter is related to what she is teaching in class. Consider what the chapter *title* says. Most people skim right over the title as if it is not important, when in fact the title is almost always a reader's first big clue about what he is expected to learn in the words that follow. What is the textbook claiming it will be telling the reader about in the pages that follow a chapter or section title? Next, pay attention to the *sub-headings* that start each section—again, a further clue. Writers chunk information under sub-headings and whatever falls under a sub-heading is meant to give the reader more information about that topic area. If the reader reviews each sub-heading in a chapter and is able to explain it out loud (to himself or someone else) then there is a good chance he is understanding the main ideas in that section. If, however, a reader is struggling to summarize the information that will be found under a sub-heading, then he probably has not learned the information well enough yet. For example, if one wanted to explain the main idea(s) under "Reading a Chapter" in this chapter, what could be said? It isn't sufficient to repeat the sub-section title—"Oh, that's about reading a chapter." What are the key suggestions that this section is making about how to learn from books? "This section is suggesting that a reader pay attention to chapter *titles* and *sub-headings*; if the reader can't summarize the information under a sub-heading then he probably doesn't understand it yet." This is the level of summary a student should be able to do if he really is understanding what a section says.

HOW TO BETTER UNDERSTAND THE SUB-SECTIONS OF A CHAPTER
When considering how to learn from the sub-sections within a chapter, no one method will work for everyone; adaptations will depend on a student's disability and learning style. One option is for the student to quickly read a paragraph and look for *key words* that indicate what the main idea is in a paragraph. When I use this method I'm looking for key words and phrases that the teacher has used in class, or words that are part of definitions and are either **in bold** or *italicized*. Using this method I find it useful to write key words in the margin next to a paragraph to reinforce that idea in my mind. Other times I will underline that key word or idea within the paragraph. I prefer to underline ideas in pencil, because I find the colors of highlighters can actually distract me from words. Not everyone

works best with pencil underlining. I worked with one young woman whose mind worked best with facts when she highlighted different kinds of ideas in different colors. A key word or definition would be one color, an example would be in a different color, etc. While her book looked beautiful but confusing to me, this method worked very well for her learning. She could quickly find where definitions and other important information was. Use pencil, highlighter, and margin notes so that they will aid in reviewing the main ideas and key words in paragraphs and sections of a book.

If working with words is more labor intensive for a reader, then she should try the method of paying closer attention to the opening line of each paragraph; this first sentence usually tells the reader the main point of the paragraph. What follows in the rest of the paragraph will further explain that idea. Sometimes it can be useful to then skip to the last or ending line of the paragraph, which will either summarize what the paragraph said or will act as a transition into the next idea being explained. Sometimes reading the first and last line of paragraphs will allow a student to learn the main idea of a sub-section and then she can choose one or two paragraphs to focus on if she needs more information about that sub-section.

Some readers have disabilities that will keep them from clearly retaining all the information within a paragraph—they are best served by pulling out the biggest main point of a paragraph; they may benefit from then writing that idea down in the margin next to the paragraph. Don't be surprised to discover that some paragraphs have many words but basically contain one idea; writers try and explain a main idea and sometimes they can get very wordy doing that, or use really long examples that do not add much information but are rather complicated to mentally process. Most professors are not interested in the smaller details in a textbook; they want students to take away the main points. Again, the biggest test of whether the reader understands a section in a book is the verbal test—or substitute writing for stating out loud—giving a summary of the main points. Based on the summary, another person should be able to learn the main point. Only a few people arrive at the point of learning information by reading every paragraph very closely over and over—this method is too time consuming. For example, the main idea of this paragraph has been that most paragraphs have a main idea. After reading this paragraph once a reader could write that idea in the margin, or underline it, and move on.

Textbooks are also making increasing use of sidebars and margin notes to further assist students in realizing what the main important points are in sections and to further explain ideas. Sidebars and areas of texts that are blocked off within the chapter will provide examples and further information about the main idea in that section of the book. A reader should look for the main themes and ideas and make sure they understand them well enough that they could be explained to another person. The real test of what a reader has actually learned comes back to what he can teach another person.

If the only way a student can feel comfortable that she is learning what she needs to is by carefully reading a section of a book several times over, then this may be a very good indicator that she should limit the number of classes she takes each semester. I always suggest to students who are taking difficult, text-heavy classes and also live with a processing disorder or disability that significantly impacts their ability to read, that they take fewer classes and perhaps even consider not taking a full class load. A student with a qualifying disability can be given an accommodation which allows the university to recognize the student as full-time for the purpose of housing (they can still live on campus in a dorm) even though the number of classes they are taking is below the normal full-time credit load. Some students are very capable of university work as long as they adjust the number of classes they take which involve the kind of information processing that they struggle with.

Learning from Lectures

How a student learns from a lecture overlaps with what a student should be learning from the textbook.

Note to Students

- Before going to class look over the assigned reading for the day.

- Try to identify key ideas and words before heading into a lecture.

- Textbooks try and give big hints about key words and tend to either **bold** them or *italicize* these words to indicate their importance.

- Do not try to memorize key words at this point.

- Read over material so that if the professor mentions key words in class they sound familiar.

Look and listen for key words:

- In class, listen for key ideas and words that the professor discusses.

- A reader who has looked the reading over with attention should hear some words repeated from their reading.

- What does the professor write on the board or place in their slides for presentation in class? These are ideas that the professor thinks are important. Some professors will provide an outline or slides online before class—print these and bring them to class to aid note-taking.

After classes for the day are over but before too much time has passed, a student should look at the assigned reading for the class again. At this point the student should be starting to see a pattern of clues. Key words that the book emphasizes, key words the professor said, ideas that both are discussing. A student does not need to worry about memorizing every bit of information from a chapter, however, he should be able to explain to another person the main points or ideas from the chapter and the professor's lecture. By doing the reading and attending the lecture a student should have a reasonably clear idea of what the professor is considering the most important points each day.

The absolute best resource for a student with a question is the teacher. If a student does not understand what happened in class then she should go to the professor's office during the posted office hours; office hours can be found in the syllabus that the professor gives out at the beginning of the semester. Occasionally professors will have to be out of their office at a time when they would normally be there—this is when using email is important. A student can email a professor and politely request a meeting time. If the class has a Teaching Assistant then this is another person a student can bring their questions to. If a student is struggling with homework then she should also look for a learning center on campus where tutors are available to work with students on the homework.

Study Aids and Preparing for Exams

Many professors are trying to clarify their teaching by providing outlines, slides, or other types of study guides online. Each university now uses an online system to provide students access to assignments, grades, and sometimes discussion boards for a class. The system varies from school to school—Blackboard and Canvas are two of the more widely used of the available systems. If a student is not sure which system his school uses, he should make inquiries with his academic advisor or disability support person. To be as successful as possible a student needs to develop the habit of checking what each professor has posted for their class in the online information format for the class—and check their email for updates from their professors. Professors will post updates to homework and assignments; they may change deadlines or expand on the information they have provided for an assignment. Some professors will also enable a discussion feature that allows students to share questions or further discuss a topic raised in class—these discussions can again be useful in gaining more clues about the information that a student is meant to be learning in the class. Some professors also make a portion of the student's grade dependent on participating in online discussion formats by posting or answering questions. Professors will indicate that this is part of the class expectation in the syllabus for the class.

Use Study Guides when Provided

Many professors will give a class a study guide before an exam. Again, one has to put some time and effort into making use of a study guide but students who faithfully use these usually do much better than students who do not. For example, a professor may hand out 20 study questions before an exam and tell students that five of those questions will be the exam. Some students will try and play the odds and choose to prepare for only those questions which are most likely to be on the exam...*in their opinion*. I have lost count of the number of students I've worked with who have gambled this way and lost. I also work with numerous students who forgo social events while preparing for exams, take time to answer all 20 study questions and then do well on the exam because they were well prepared. Interestingly, the students who are most likely to enter a STEM school recognizing they have to work harder to get information out of a class—those who have AD/HD, dyslexia, and learning disabilities—are the students most likely to use study guides like this and be successful. Students in school who managed to rely primarily on their intelligence and memory are the students most likely to start struggling in university because they either do not make use of study guides or they make very limited use of them; they also have little practice studying. Students who have never developed the habit of studying before university struggle to learn how to study once they arrive at university. They simply have not developed the necessary practices and do not know where to begin.

Developing Study Habits

Like all habits, developing studying as a habit is something best done while a child is still living at home. A family can work with teachers to ensure that their student is developing a routine that will facilitate learning in the future. How well a student is doing with studying should not be judged solely by his grades. If a student is frequently bored in class, maintains good grades yet seldom brings homework home, then the student is not learning to study. Some students do not need to study to obtain good grades but they will eventually need to study if they are to be successful in the required university classes they *do not* have an aptitude for or interest in.

Note to Parents

There are steps a family can take to ensure their student is developing study habits that will lead to later success. Learning to study should go hand in glove with learning to keep schoolwork organized.

- Teach students to keep information about different classes in separate notebooks.

- Provide students with a unique coloured notebook for each class in the semester, for example, red for math, blue for geography, etc.

- When possible use notebooks that have a folder pocket for holding handouts from the teacher.

- Teach students to organize their handouts and notes by date, which will help keep them organized by class discussions and topic areas.

- Teach students that, even if they do not write notes during class, at the end of the day they need to take at least ten minutes per class they attended to write down what they remember the teacher discussing in class that day.

If a student does not find it necessary to study for classes, then a family can teach study habits by helping the student learn about topics outside of school. Start with topic areas that are of interest to the student.

- Discuss how one learns about something new.

- Show the student how to find books and resources in the library, on the internet, and how to judge what is a reliable source.

- Sit down with the student and together write a brief report of what has been learned.

- As the student grows, help her learn about a topic each semester that is *not* as interesting to her but that has some practical value like how to research which brand of tire to buy for her car or what to consider when choosing a university.

Students who can only study what interests them risk failing mandatory classes in university—everyone needs to learn how to learn about things that do not fascinate them.

Tutors

I've discovered in my own life and as a teacher that most people have at least one topic that they are very strong in and one topic where they have to work a lot harder just to get by. Some people may be able to process numbers in their sleep but struggle with writing a paragraph; other people are able to write but have trouble picturing something in their mind and need to see a picture to aid their learning. There are a number of learning styles and strengths. In a competitive STEM university it is very likely that a student will eventually encounter a required class that they struggle with. It seems to happen to everyone eventually.

If a student is fortunate, then there will be a *learning center* or other academic support service available on campus that specializes in the kind of information that they need. At my current school each department operates their own learning center to support the classes they teach. Not everyone, however, finds a learning center environment conducive to their learning. Other times, a learning center may not be available to provide support for a more advanced course. In such cases a professor and teaching assistant are the student's first resources for information. If the student finds they require even more support, then it is time to look for a *qualified tutor*.

I prefer to look for private tutors first amongst the staff of the learning centers; a learning center will always have a person in charge of staffing. Ask this person if they can help you find a tutor to work with outside of learning center hours and discuss what you can afford to pay for this service. If you cannot afford to pay, then ask if the learning center is aware of any student organizations that offer free tutoring.

Sometimes student organizations will offer tutoring as a community service. A number of universities have someone on their staff who is responsible for organizing these student organizations. This is another person one can make inquiries of when looking for tutoring that is offered as a service to the community. It may also be possible to find out which organizations on campus include members in the field of study that a student is struggling with, be that math, physics, communication, etc. Ask the organizer of student groups if he is aware of any group or individual offering tutoring.

Every campus also has a *student-run newspaper* that has a section where students can run advertisements. If a student is uncomfortable approaching any of these other sources of tutors, then an advertisement for a tutor can be placed in the campus newspaper. It is helpful to specify the level of the class the tutor is needed for, so that potential tutors know the kind of information a student needs assistance with. If someone responds to the advertisement, clarify which classes they have taken in the applicable field and what their grades have been.

Finally, there is the *internet*. One can run a search for tutors in the geographic area that specialize in different fields of study. Sometimes a professor or graduate student in the area will be offering tutoring in their free time. Otherwise-qualified individuals (retired teachers, etc.) will also offer tutoring. In these cases a student should ask for references and should only agree to meet the tutor in a public space such as the school or community library. Like any other interview, it is necessary to inquire into what qualifies the individual to be offering the tutoring they offer. Also clarify rates, the length of the tutoring session, and the frequency of sessions during your initial conversation.

Taking Tests

Professors grade students on how well they show them what they have learned. Some professors have developed better methods for discovering this than others and I will discuss this further in Chapter 7. An important key to being successful in university is recognizing that different professors will be looking for different levels of understanding from students. A few professors will ask students to give them specific details out of massive amounts of information. Most professors, though, want to see an indication that students are learning the main concepts in a class. Does a student know the main formulas, theories, equations?

Professors will also have different ways of grading (or "valuing") what students show them. Some professors really value students talking in class and will base part of a student's grade on her participation and/or attendance. Sometimes students will be given a range of ways to show knowledge including group projects, presentations, and papers. Other professors, particularly those teaching large lecture classes, will grade students entirely on tests that use Scantron answer sheets (I tend to call them "bubble-in" sheets—you indicate your answers to questions by using a pencil to fill in the little bubbles). Scantron sheets can be fed through a computer for grading and this is much more time-feasible when a professor has hundreds or thousands of students in a class. In a large lecture class it usually isn't realistic to allow students any other way to show what they are learning except perhaps for a laboratory section attached to the class.

5

Professors' and Students' Classroom Behavior

I heard a deep sigh from the professor on the phone. "You know, Christy, I was able to work around his sudden need to jump up in the middle of my lecture—even when he bursts out of the room. But this classroom isn't very big and when he started lying on the floor at the front of the class...well, I need to be able to move without tripping over him."

The young man being discussed had made his way through high school constantly accompanied by a personal aide. Now that he was in university and without an aide, I was getting regular calls and emails about his behavior. He was prone to verbal outbursts and loud mumbling when his fellow students talked or gave presentations; he made it clear to other students that he found their intelligence lacking. The professor on the phone was one of the few people for whom the student had shown any respect. In fact, the student told me this was actually his favorite class and faculty member. I knew if his behavior in his favorite class was this disruptive, things must be getting nearly unbearable in his other classes.

When is Behavior Beyond Tolerable?

The young man who no longer had an aide had been to my office fairly regularly. Unlike some students with socially challenging behavior who tend to isolate themselves in their dorm rooms, this young man started to seek me out when he was upset. I walked him into Counseling Services and made sure he had regular appointments.

At least, I made sure he booked regular appointments. He was very hit or miss about attending these meetings. When he was upset about the behavior of others, or uncertain about why some people acted or spoke the way they did, he would come bursting into my office, often before the person at the front desk in the reception area could stop him or announce his arrival. My office door slamming back against the wall was my notice that he had arrived. When I pointed out that slamming doors was socially unacceptable he would apologize and on a good day would remember not to slam the door on his way out.

As the increasing reports of his declining behavior in classrooms started to reach me, I decided to accompany him to several classes to see what we were dealing with. I made sure we arrived at the first class five minutes before it started so that I could explain to the professor why I was sitting in. The professor had just started his lesson for the day when the young man bolted out of his chair and began pacing at the back of the room. He then suddenly collapsed in a chair like a sack of wheat and after a minute his feet were up on the table; I motioned for him to put his feet down and he complied. As he became more distressed by what he seemed to consider stupid questions from his fellow students, he suddenly leapt to his feet mumbling and left the room. He was gone for over ten minutes. He returned to loudly re-enter the class just minutes before it was to end. In the next class I had the opportunity to witness him give part of a group presentation and I winced on behalf of the rest of his group. When anyone else spoke he mumbled in disagreement or made somewhat audible comments like, "Well that's obvious" or "We could have just read the book." When it was his turn to present he talked down to the audience in a rapid, condescending manner while also going into far greater detail about events than the presentation warranted. In a really horrible way it was almost funny—like a bad situation comedy on television where a person's behavior is so over the top it does not seem real. Unfortunately, it was all too real. Even worse, afterwards his professor told me the student's behavior had been a bit quieter than normal with me present and watching him.

Eventually we reached the point where the student had to be dropped from some of his classes because his behavior was beyond what the professor and other students were willing or able to tolerate. When he enrolled for a second semester of classes, we once again found we had to force him to drop some classes partway through the semester. After all, the other students were every bit as entitled to their education as this student was and in university there are rules that each student must meet. This student's behavior was starting to transgress the school's Code of Conduct. Every university has a Code of Conduct, which sets out rules such as banning drinking in rooms that are rented by under-age students and banning the damaging of university property. If these rules are broken then the possible outcomes include fines, suspension, or expulsion for behavior that is not acceptable in classrooms, dorm rooms, and other areas of university-owned property. The Code of Conduct also has rules that apply to students' behavior while they are enrolled in school but off campus. Students do not always realize that getting in trouble off campus can still lead to charges under the Code of Conduct.

This student's conduct was not just becoming problematic in classes, he also was having difficulty with peers in his dorm hallway. He repeatedly exploded verbally because he felt they were too loud. He was very sensitive to the fact that a student in the hall near him seemed to be teasing him and deliberately trying to provoke him. Both students ended up being written up in incident reports—one for bordering on bullying behavior, the other for reacting by cornering the student and screaming at him in a manner that frightened other people in the hall. In his second semester we tried putting the student on a floor with more mature students who were all in single rooms. While he found this setting a slight improvement he now refused to acknowledge his fellow students by saying so much as hello when they passed him in the hall and greeted him. By the beginning of his second year this young man was on a behavior agreement with Conduct Services, the branch of the Dean of Students' office on our campus that works with students who have violated the Code of Conduct. Partway into his third semester, this young man broke the contract by storming through a series of offices, intentionally punching over a display, slamming doors, loudly swearing as he stomped through public spaces—he was taking a long way around to my office—and scaring some of the staff to the point where they were about to call the police, when I came out of my office to discover the source of the noise. One of my colleagues, a former Marine, was ahead of me on the way into the waiting area and when the student saw us both entering the room, he exited out a side door, circled around and went into my office, slamming the door with such force he shattered a mirror that was hanging on the back of it.

This was the final straw for Conduct Services. I called the young man's parents and told them they would have to come and pick him up, because he was being suspended for the remainder of the semester. His mother's response? "But he was doing so much better!" Ironically, the young man had improved in his time with us but it was too little too late. We simply did not have enough time to get his behavior and conduct to the point where it should have been before he arrived on campus. I regretted that due to their own challenges, his parents had not better prepared this young man for the transition into independent living.

I am sharing this young man's story at this point because I want to make something clear. It was only because he encountered several professors that were so tolerant of his behavior and willing to work with him that this young man was able to complete even one semester of university. The professor who taught this student's favorite class continued to work with him through his entire time enrolled here and I think this professor deserves a great deal of the credit for the student making it as far as he did. Each of the three semesters the student would sign up for a class taught by this professor and those classes were always the highlight of his semester. They were also some of the few classes he could be counted on to attend and pass.

Professors' Expectations

Behavior does not have to reach the point of students charging in and out of class or lying on the floor to be seen as disrespectful by professors. Even more troubling for those who teach is what appears to be a trend in increasingly disrespectful comportment from students. Classroom behavior, emails, conversations—professors are feeling overwhelmed by the areas where students are becoming ruder and apparently less capable of appropriate interactions. Students are decreasingly prepared to act in a mature manner and fail to realize how important good relationships with professors can be. Working with professors dramatically increases the likelihood that a student will be successful in university. Disrespecting a professor increases the probability that a student will be shown little or no forgiveness for errors, absences, or misunderstandings that result in errors in homework and exams. Students might also be surprised to learn how often their grade is on the very edge between grades—one point between going up or down an entire letter grade. Having a good working relationship with a professor increases the likelihood that the grade will be bumped up rather than kept at the lower level. Behavior, participation, and comportment can all affect a student's grade; they also indicate if a student is becoming any better prepared to work in a professional environment.

Professors have worked and studied a long, hard time to reach the point they are at in the educational system. Unlike some liberal arts professors who may be expected to primarily seek employment in a university, at a STEM university many professors have knowledge that would allow them to make money in the private sector at significantly higher rates than teaching provides.

Rather than capitalizing on their knowledge, professors at STEM universities instead choose to work with students so that the information they have is passed on to future generations. Many value research and mentoring people who are entering their field of expertise. In return they expect to be addressed with respect and to have their titles used when first meeting new people, that means referring to them as "Doctor" or "Professor" rather than "Mr.," "Mrs.," or "Ms." One should not assume that one can be on a first-name basis with a professor just because other students are; a student should wait for the professor to extend an invitation to be this informal with her. Remember, a professor may have given up a certain degree of economic gain in order to teach; in return they expect the level of specialized knowledge they have to be acknowledged by students showing them some courtesy.

Personal comportment

The professor's tone was alarmed. "This student demanded, *demanded* that I alter his grade! He raised his voice to me and wouldn't even *listen* when I tried to explain how he'd earned the grade he was given." This was a "horror tale" being told by a professor to a group of colleagues; everyone's head was nodding. Each professor had encountered such a scenario.

"The sense of entitlement amongst students is unbelievable," another commented.

Everyone in the room had heard and was tired of the sentiment students sometimes express, "I'm paying for this education—you work for me!"

I have always worked at public universities. While students do indeed pay a portion of their educational costs, what they fail to realize is that so do I, the faculty, and the rest of the staff. As a taxpayer working in this state, I help fund the university—not to mention all the infrastructure supporting the university like highways and road maintenance crews, which help make it possible for students to continue to attend school. While state funding has declined over the years, it is still part of what makes offering an education to students possible. No student or their family independently pays for everything that makes educating them possible. Private donors have built buildings and contributed equipment; grants for research not only fund research but often the labs, equipment and even work that is available for students; individuals and corporations fund specific professorships or "chairs" allowing universities to hire a professor they otherwise would not be able to pay. Taxpayers are also the source of the money that the government makes available for student loans and grants. Everyone at a public university has a partially subsidized education and most students at private universities do as well. It is not accurate then, to say that you are "paying for your education" as if you are buying a kitchen appliance—there is no warranty, no money back, and no service-on-demand with a university education but then, you aren't fully paying for everything that is part of that education either.

It is also important to realize that families who teach their children basic social etiquette are helping prepare them for greater success both in university and in their future professional lives. Remember, no matter what area of specialization a student studies in, when it is time to become employed, employers will be looking for: (1) an ability to work with others, (2) an ability to communicate clearly. As our society's commerce, science, and technology industries are increasingly run on a global scale our citizens are increasingly called on to interact with professionals/clients from other nations. There are a number of guides available to help people know more about the cultures and customs of social groups outside one's own. Business etiquette begins with the same foundational concepts that ought to be used in a university when students are addressing faculty.

Note to Students

Dealing with non-family members works best if you practice treating people with respect:

- Do not raise your voice or use an angry tone.

- Say please when asking for something—including requests for someone else's time.

- Say thank you when someone gives you something— including their time.

- Do not swear or tell people they are stupid or otherwise name-call; not everyone will be as clever as you are but pointing this out never benefits you.

Appropriate Tone in Email

With the increase in social media use, the lines between formal and informal communication are becoming ever more blurred, that is to say that people can fall into the habit of emailing their professors and university staff in a tone that is more appropriate for exchanging messages with friends or family.

This is an example of an actual email I received from a student:

"Am I able to get my money back for dropping classes?"

That was the entire content of the email. As someone who teaches Technical Communication I could fill several pages detailing all the ways this email is wrong. Instead, I will explain the correct format for an email.

Salutation: Professor (or Dr.) Oslund

Reference or reminder of subject being discussed: As you may recall, on Monday, September 20, we met to discuss my medical problems and if I should drop my classes or take a reduced credit load.

Summation of reason for email: I have decided I need to drop my classes. Will I get any money back if I have a medical withdrawal now?

Closing: Thank you for your help

Your name: Bob Robertson

Or put all together and it looks like this:

> Dr. Oslund,
>
> As you may recall, on Monday, September 20, we met to discuss my medical problems and if I should drop my classes or take a reduced credit load. I have decided I need to drop my classes. Will I get any money back if I have a medical withdrawal now?
>
> Thank you for your help,
> Bob Robertson

Note to students

When emailing, just like when speaking to someone in person, one will get further by remembering to be polite:

- Use the name and title of the person being contacted.

- Remind the person of the context for your communication— are you referring to something that has a previous communication history? If not, it will be necessary to explain why the person is being contacted; what is the purpose of the email?

- Give the main reason for the current email.

- Thank the reader for their time.

- Include your name in the closing—a closing also indicates that the message is ending.

Appropriate Phone Etiquette

I find it ironic that people have become so comfortable with phones that we often fail to stop and consider our phone manners—or lack of manners on the phone as the case may be. A basic refresher course in how to conduct a conversation by phone would probably be useful for many people; it is particularly necessary for young people who have grown up phone-in-hand, having conversations primarily with family and friends.

There are some key things to remember when talking to university faculty and staff on the phone:

- We do not necessarily recognize people's voices—*the caller should always identify themselves by name*, for example, "This is Bob Robertson."

- Faculty and staff know many people with similar first names so it is not helpful when a caller only uses their first name; it is better to use a full name: "This is Bob Robertson."

- Faculty and staff have many, many people, places, and things taking up space in their minds—*please remind the recipient of a call of the reason for the call*: "We've been talking about tearing up the parking lot and planting a field of sunflowers where the freshmen park. I'm calling to let you know that there is equipment on the way to the lot to start this project and wanted to know if you wanted to be there."

- Faculty and staff may not be prepared for the phone call or the information in the phone call: "Bob, I have the entire freshman class in my office right now, could I please call you back in ten minutes? And Bob—don't let the equipment start working."

I currently work in the Dean of Students' office. It seems to be a daily occurrence that we get phone calls from students who do not identify themselves, or who use only their first names, "Hi, this is Sue." They do not clearly state why they are calling but will start firing questions at the person who answers the phone. Often people then hang up without saying "good-bye" or "thank you." It doesn't take long answering phones on a switchboard like this to get fairly tired of having to deal with people. Professors are responsible for assigning grades, and staff are responsible for handling basically all other aspects of a student's university life from housing to permission to repeat classes that a student has already failed several times. Alienating staff or faculty by being rude on the phone does not serve anyone well. Practicing basic phone etiquette can help students more smoothly and quickly resolve any necessary phone calls.

Faculty can be Disabled Too

As I looked at the two faculty members seated at the table with me I couldn't help but be reminded of our students. One had his shirt buttoned to the top, his hair slicked down, his arms stiffly folded. The other had hair that didn't appear to have seen a brush in several days, a faded shirt that might have been mis-buttoned, and had finally flopped into his chair after wandering in and out of the room several times just as the meeting was about to start; he rocked several times in his chair before glancing at me then glancing away. Neither was comfortable with direct eye contact. One was stiff, the other distracted. They were combined in purpose though.

"We need you to give us more rules," the serious professor quietly stated.

His colleague was a little louder, "These people don't know what they're doing [he was talking about the students]. Can we just send them all back to you?"

Do you know a student with a strong understanding of a specialized field in science, technology, math, or engineering? Does this student feel they know this subject well enough to tell others about it? Does this student like routine that lasts for weeks on end? Can they deal with small changes in routine when they know exactly when to expect those changes? Can they focus in myopic detail on some knowledge while being oblivious to where their keys or phone are? Then this student may grow up to be a professor at a STEM university.

Once people stop to think about it, it really does make perfect sense that the same things that draw young people to the STEM fields can keep them in the STEM fields. I often suspect that there is a much larger percentage of invisibly disabled people around the conference tables at faculty meetings than there are present in any classroom at any STEM university. Which is why I am generally not surprised to find professors who have the exact same issues and expectations as the students I work with. Recognizing that many professors were once the (possibly undiagnosed) invisibly disabled student will help a family and their student better prepare for the transition to a STEM university. As a family you can also begin to understand the importance of teaching students to create routines of behavior for their classroom performance.

- Professors want to know what to expect—make sure they know about accommodations from the beginning of the semester.

- Professors believe that their areas of interest are important— if students treat their subject matter with disrespect the professor will be hurt, angry, or insulted (none of which are good for the offending student).

- Professors may never have known what it was to struggle with a class in their field—a student may need tutors or learning centers if a professor can't simplify their explanations.

- Professors may not be organized and may be forgetful— students should put agreements and important information in writing and keep a copy.

- Professors may be very literal in their understanding of the world—students and their families should never assume anyone shares a sense of humor; be respectful and to the point in communication.

At the same time, as I previously noted, many of the professors who teach here could have chosen to take a more lucrative route and work in private industry. Instead, they have chosen to pursue a career in the university. Others have spent time in the private sector and teaching at a STEM university is a second career which was chosen precisely because the person believes in the value of education. This is another universal feature I find at our STEM university—the people who work here believe that education matters, and that what they are teaching matters. They have a genuine interest in helping students become interested in and excited by their ideas.

The biggest complaint I hear from professors? Students do not come and talk to them more often. They welcome interest in their work, their research, their topic areas. While not all professors are equally good at explaining their complex ideas, they all have an interest in sharing their knowledge. Most are willing to spend time explaining and going through examples with students. When they see students willing to put time and effort into what they teach, they are generally very willing to give such students further explanations and examples.

I will use myself as an example. As a graduate student working on my Master's degree, I was required to take a formal logic class and obtain at least a B or 3 GPA (on 4 scale) to meet the requirements for my degree. I had not yet been diagnosed as dyslexic, I just knew that the formal logic formulas I was expected to memorize and use were virtually impossible to hold in my head. I had taken a logic class as an undergraduate and by working on every extra credit assignment the teacher offered me, I had done well. This more advanced formal logic just seemed like too much.

The first time I took the class, I waited until the last day to drop it, hoping to learn as much as I could; the professor took me aside and told me, "There's just no way you can pass."

The second time I took the class I knew I had to complete it. The class was only offered once a year and I was in my second and final year of the program. I had a different professor this time and he encouraged me to come to his office hours and ask questions. As he saw me earnestly work through a problem he decided that maybe more practice would help me. He gave me additional homework. I did it. Not well, but to the best of my ability. He began to tutor me outside his office hours. Soon we were meeting twice a week outside of office hours as he continued to provide additional teaching and I continued to work my heart out to limited results.

I was so proud when I got my final exam back. I had gotten my B with one point to spare. The professor confided in me, "I've never seen anyone work so hard—I was going to give you that B no matter what. But I was really pleased to see you earn it—you even had a point to spare!"

I did my classwork, my homework, and extra pages of homework. Because I never quit trying this particular professor never quit trying to help me. I was fortunate to find a professor so willing to work with a student who others would have given up on as hopeless. This has been a repeating theme in my education though. When I struggle with a subject but show how hard I am willing to work on it, I eventually find a teacher who is willing to stand by me through this struggle and help me learn.

6

Work Study Jobs, Resumes, and Class Study Groups

With the increasing cost of education, most families will use loans to help pay for their child's education. Additionally, many students will qualify for work study opportunities on campus. Basically, every department and area of campus such as Facilities (the people who keep up the buildings) and Dining Services (including the stores and coffee shops on campus) hire students. The jobs available to students fall into two categories: regular part time employment—the department has budgeted for the entire student salary to come out of their funds; and work study—part of the student's wage is paid by their financial aid package and therefore the department that hires the student doesn't have to pay as much out of their budget. Work study employment is an additional type of financial aid that is available to students who qualify.[1]

Each college will have several different sources of privately sponsored scholarships and grants that are available due to the generosity of people in the community and alum. All accredited schools within the US and Canada work with their respective federal funding agents so that qualifying students can receive federal loans. Students and their families will have to file paperwork to be eligible for any form of aid and each school provides information about this process. These days, every college has a website, which is a good place to start researching the types of aids that a school has in

---

1   Every college has an office that specializes in financial aid applications and questions. These are the best people to talk to about what an individual student will be eligible for at that institution—aid and costs vary from school to school.

addition to federal aid. For students who need to practice studying or conducting research (Chapter 4), this would also make an excellent research topic—what kinds of financial aid are available to them at the different schools they are interested in?

Although work study jobs are part of a financial aid package, in order to get such a job a student usually has to do more than financially qualify. On our campus for example, work study jobs have to be applied for just as one has to apply for any other part-time job: a resume needs to be sent in and at least one job interview will be necessary. On our campus, the Career Services Department sponsors a website that lists all the jobs open on campus and there is an online form that students must fill out to apply for work. After a student applies for a job, they must then take part in a job interview. The whole system has been designed to give students practice in applying and interviewing for jobs; this is knowledge and practice they will benefit from in the future when they have graduated and are seeking full-time employment.

Job Experience for a Resume

Every year I volunteer with Career Services to review resumes for students who will be seeking employment or a co-op or internship. Co-ops and internships are work experiences with a company that does the kind of work a student is interested in having when they graduate, for example, working in a plant that manufactures cars, working in a veterinarian clinic, assisting in a research laboratory, etc. At our institution, a co-op refers to unpaid work that a student is doing as part of a class he is taking—the work is part of the student's learning experience; an internship is paid work with a company while a student is not enrolled in a class, for example, a summer job, or working for a semester or even a year with a company to gain experience *before* a student has completed their education and graduated with a degree. Internships are not only the best way for a student to discover if they really enjoy a field of work, or to clarify what specific job in a field they would like, they also usually offer the kinds of hands-on experience that will lead to future job offers when the student does graduate.

Every year as I assist students with preparing their resumes so that they can apply for co-ops and internships, I meet students who have had no job experience, very little work experience, or have worked only for a family-owned business. It is vitally important that these students have opportunities to work with others before they graduate. Most of these students would have greatly benefited from opportunities to volunteer and gain some knowledge and skills related to working with others before they arrived on campus. While some students live with disabilities that make seeking work a challenge, there are always opportunities to gain working experience by volunteering. Nursing homes, hospitals, libraries, animal shelters, Habitat for Humanity,[2] sports and recreation groups, community programs, and a family's religious organization can all provide opportunities for young people, perhaps originally working alongside their parents, to start building knowledge and skills that will be important for creating a resume that will then help them gain further job opportunities and be better prepared to work with others. The same skills needed for working with others in an employment context would also benefit a student when it is time for him to do classroom group work.

I will again use myself as an example. Growing up I held numerous odd jobs including spending an afternoon sorting worms, a great deal of time babysitting, a summer cleaning cabins—basically I tried not to turn down any reasonable opportunity that I could find to gain work experience. My first teaching job was facilitated not so much by my history of paid employment as by some volunteering I'd done through my church. The department that first hired me to teach was desperate for a teacher who had spent some time with young people; the department had many job applicants who while all educationally qualified to teach the material, mainly had zero experience working with students. I rose to the top of that pile because I had several years' experience volunteering as a youth leader in my community. I was the best suited in an underqualified teaching pool. My reward was becoming the teacher for a class of 60 students after I had an entire week of training. That, however, is another story and I confess, I was lucky to get that week of training.

It is important to think about preparing students to work with others before they arrive at university. The ability to not just tolerate but communicate with other people is going to affect a student's

---

2 Habitat for Humanity is a volunteer, non-profit group that builds affordable, safe housing around the world: www.habitat.org.

potential for doing well in classes where they will have to work with classmates; in finding work including work study; and in eventually being hired after graduation. Education will not be the boon a family hopes for, if their child is unable to work to some degree with their colleagues and classmates. This includes being able to work with those who do not share their educational background and interests.

Do not expect a university to teach the capacity to work with others at a foundational level. A student needs to arrive at university with some capacity to work with others already developed. This may mean that a student needs to actually take a year or two between leaving high school and entering university if she is particularly struggling in the area of working with others. It is far better for a person to develop a working capacity to co-operate with others before she arrives at university if she is going to maximize her potential in university. It will also be very emotionally and psychology defeating if a student should complete their university education only to discover that she is so lacking in the ability to work with others or communicate that she cannot find employment because she struggles to even manage a job interview.

If paid employment is not a current practical solution for a student, then remember that work skills can also be learned through *volunteering*.

School and social groups can also provide opportunities for practicing skills that will help build a resume. If a student is particularly strong in a subject, he could volunteer through his school to work with other students as a tutor or homework buddy. Some schools even offer learning centers for math, writing, or other subjects that are staffed by students. My Canadian high school had a tutoring class that students could sign up for as a credit; I received credits for tutoring other students in English and worked with tutors for assistance with my math and chemistry. In fact, if it hadn't been for the assistance of my lab partner/tutor in chemistry I would never have understood anything that happened in that class. This later tutoring arrangement was an informal agreement we worked out because I struggled with chemistry and my lab partner wanted someone to assist her with her English papers. This kind of co-operation is particularly beneficial for students who get to exchange roles as tutor/tutee. The knowledge and skills can still be used on a resume. For example, under the heading "volunteer activity" a student could list, "peer-tutored chemistry student." Better yet, a student can volunteer to help several students, or lead a study group. The work experience then could be placed under the category "leadership" and could list, "organized and led a peer-study group of grade eleven chemistry students—scheduled meeting times and places—facilitated homework discussion for a group of [*number*] students."

Note to students

If you lack work experience then you can gain experience through volunteering. Steps you can take:

- Find an organization or group that has goals you consider worth working towards.

- Volunteer at least once a week with the group—be punctual and responsible—treat this like a paid job.

- As you become more comfortable with the group, increase the level of responsibility you take on.

- Volunteer to help work as part of a leadership team—this kind of experience is very important to future employers. You can help organize a seasonal event, fundraiser, etc.

- Seek out opportunities to work with people who have different backgrounds from you—experience working with a diverse group of people is very valuable to employers.

- If the group you initially volunteer with is made up of "similar" people (e.g. white, middle-class, Scandinavian Lutherans) then create the personal goal of volunteering with an additional group that is more diverse, such as Habitat for Humanity, the Salvation Army, a local food bank, etc.

Preparing for Work Study Opportunities

If a student is preparing to leave home for college, then there are several things he can do to get ready for work study. It may help to review with a student's current teachers how he is doing with group work. Can he work with others? Where does he run into challenges?

Is he able to make eye contact at least briefly so that a person feels he is directly addressing them? Is he able to shake hands and make an appropriate social comment, such as "Good morning," "How do you do," "Hello, I'm…"

Handshaking and Greetings

Young women and young men need to be able to shake someone else's hand in social contexts because this is considered correct social etiquette for business and professional settings.

Note to Students
How to shake hands:

- Use your full hand—not just the finger tips—unless you have arthritis or a disability that prevents this.

- Apply just enough pressure so that the other person is aware of your hand without being hurt by it or having their own hand squeezed.

- Remember—the other person may have arthritis, fibromyalgia, or other physical complications.

- STEM fields do not prize handshakes that are a show of strength but they do value the appearance that you are able to meet basic social expectations.

It is valuable to practice handshaking with a student and then have the student practice with other people who are able to provide appropriate feedback, for example, "That's a good handshake" or "That is too tight" or "You need to actually touch my hand for it to count as a handshake." The student could also practice the correct social responses when shaking hands, for example saying what is socially expected given the circumstances such as time of day and whether this is a first meeting, or greeting someone they already know. Parents could work with a student on making at least brief eye contact with the person they are greeting. This is a skill which will be very useful when the student eventually has job interviews.

Job interviews often begin with people who work in the Human Resources Department of a company or institution and these people look for a fairly standard set of social skills as an indication that a person has some practice working with others. HR people often see a lack of these basic social skills as a red flag that someone will have difficulty working with others.

IF A STUDENT HAS OCD OR IS WORRIED ABOUT GERMS...

If a person has obsessive compulsive disorder or otherwise finds it very difficult to touch other people, than practicing how to do so before they must is even more important. In order to relieve some of the stress of having to touch people, I suggest that a person learn to carry a small bottle of hand-sanitizer and/or wet wipes with them.

Note to students

How to subtly meet the OCD need to hand-sanitize after handshaking:

- Place a wet wipe in a pocket just before meeting people.

- When the person you've just met turns for a moment to speak to someone else, or to lead you into an interview room, reach into your pocket and wipe your hand without making a show of the process.

- Most people will find it off-putting if you immediately pull out a wet wipe or hand-sanitizer after you have touched their hand, defeating the purpose of trying to learn this social skill.

- It is preferable to have several years of practice with social skills like greetings and handshaking before arriving at college.

- If you haven't been practicing this skill set, start immediately.

In my office I keep a pump bottle of hand-sanitizer next to a box of facial tissues, both of which are out for everyone to use. I try to avoid unintentionally insulting people by hand-sanitizing immediately after shaking their hand; I will hand-sanitize after they leave my office. When I am traveling I will usually carry not only hand-sanitizer and wet wipes, but also hand-sanitizing lotion. These travel-size bottles of lotion which include sanitizer as an ingredient are a less conspicuous way of cleaning my hands after greeting people or handling items that many other people have handled. One can learn to accommodate both their OCD needs and their social obligations with practice. I am OCD and live with anxiety disorder but have managed to develop the practice of shaking hands when meeting new people and no longer find this an uncomfortable social practice—it did, however, take practice to reach this point.

Handshaking will have social significance for some individuals more than others. Those who work in STEM fields will sometimes find it necessary to work with business people, meet investors, and otherwise spend time with members of the public who are less aware of fairly commonplace circumstances such as OCD/anxiety-related reluctance to touch strangers. As a result, some people will unfairly judge a person who refuses to shake hands with them, or just touches their hand with finger tips, or immediately hand-sanitizes.

There are certain social behaviors we adapt to fit into a broader social group. Dressing in clean clothes that are appropriate to our work-station, exchanging pleasantries such as, "How are you today?", shaking hands, listening politely instead of informing someone that their story is boring you—these are all social behaviors. The ability to carry out such behaviors allows us to fit in with others; it also increases the likelihood that we will not be overlooked for a job or promotion due to a lack of social awareness. While it may not seem fair, the truth is that managers often look for far more than intelligence and even ability to do a job when they consider who to hire and who to promote. Appearances, being on time, not rushing to leave at the end of the day—these behaviors all make a difference. Like any other behaviors, the more we practice and create routines around social behavior, the more automatic and easier to carry out these behaviors tend to become. Families can work together on promoting good social behavior that will facilitate a student's successful transition into university and a career.

Writing a Resume

There are a number of sources available to provide advice on how to write a resume. It is important to remember that (1) there is more than one way to design a resume; (2) work doesn't have to be paid to be valuable; (3) there are some resume expectations that ought to be met according to the area one is working in. I'll explain each of these points in turn.

Along with my other roles, I sometimes teach Technical Communication, including how to write resumes. I've also reviewed resumes for many years, as a number of my work experiences have placed me in a position to participate in hiring committees. There are certain rules to writing a resume and different people will give different advice about which of those rules can be broken and which cannot. There is more than one way to write a resume; however, there are some points that do need to be remembered:

- A resume is about the person—their name and contact information should be the easiest pieces of information for the reader to find/see (employers read resumes before deciding who to interview).

- Titles of the sections a resume is divided into can vary; no matter the titles the idea is to show experience relevant to the position being hired.

- Experience can come from special projects, volunteering, and applied classes that have been taken.

- Experience doesn't have to be paid to count—if, however, experience is not presented in some way on the resume then a potential employer isn't going to know about it.

- Resumes work together with cover letters but *not everyone in an organization will see the cover letter.*

- Readers typically spend under one minute—and maybe as little as ten seconds—in their original viewing of a resume. A resume's design needs to make its main points clearly and cleanly. I personally have met no one on a hiring committee who wishes to read through paragraph-style resumes that explain what a person knows.

A computer search or research in the local library will find resume examples.

Note to Students

When working on a resume, if you aren't sure where or how to start, try finding five or six resumes that were written by someone with a background similar to your own trying to achieve a similar job (don't compare your resume to someone who has been out working for several years, or to someone who's applying to become a CEO—look for examples of other student resumes.)

- When reviewing sample resumes, look at the document and see what helps you find information and what makes it harder for you to understand what the writer is saying about themselves—remember these lessons as you work on your own resume.

- Keep a template of your standard resume on your computer or portable drive and be prepared to make adjustments to your resume depending on the job you are applying for.

I could go on but there are a number of books and websites that can provide detailed information about resumes if you have further questions or concerns. Seek out several references and do not take just one person's word for what makes a good resume—there are a number of opinions about resumes and it is better to learn to look at the trends, and at what traditionally works for people who are in the same field, or with similar work experience to yours. Once a student is starting to work in a particular field of study, then the standards of what makes for a good resume become dependent on the expectations of the field, so what makes for a good resume in the humanities is not the same as what makes for a good Chemical Engineering resume—even the style of how information is listed changes depending on a person's field of study. Always look at other resumes within the same field once in a specialized STEM area of study.

Section Headings

Remember, volunteer work, experience with sporting and hobby groups, team leadership experience, practice working with others—this is the kind of experience that employers are looking for and this experience does not have to have been paid for it to be valuable and on a resume. Resumes traditionally have sections with section headings but these headings do not have to be exactly the same from resume to resume. Use section headings that allow for the showcasing of work experience such as:

• volunteer work

• leadership experience

• community service.

Highlight teamwork—"teamed with 12 peers to organize community food drive" — and be specific about success—"raised x amount of money."

There are some resume expectations that ought to be met. There is a fine line between showing oneself to be creative and unique and showing oneself to be incapable of following basic rules. As many invisibly disabled people are already keenly aware, the world seems to be filled with rules that other people know and we do not. The same is true of writing a resume. Some people know the rules that need to be followed and some do not. As someone who knows the basic resume rules I am now going to share the rules that should not be broken by people in STEM fields:

• *Do not use uniquely colored paper or non-standard fonts or font sizes when creating a resume.* Typically a computer's word-processing program can be relied on to provide strong indication of what are typical fonts—word-processing programs are pre-programmed with a default font. Particularly when starting out, go with the default, for example, Times New Roman, 12 point font. There are of course some other standard choices but avoid anything that looks too atypical—whether an employer is looking for a summer employee or trying to fill an internship, they are looking for employees who show the capacity to meet expectations and follow rules. Someone needing a creative outlet for their talent should consider drawing and writing their own comic book or graphic novel; a resume is not an appropriate outlet for art work.

- A resume is also not the place to show off a whimsical side. An employer wants someone to work in a capacity that will positively affect the employer's livelihood, their ability to feed their family and keep a roof over their head. When they look at resumes they are looking for a fairly standard document that indicates someone who is likely to come in, accept training, and learn to work in the capacity that they are hired to work in. That is to say, they are looking for people who are willing to fit in, not those who need to stand out. The job is ultimately about the employer and her needs, not about the employee and his needs.

- *A resume should include a person's name and contact information—a phone number where he can be reached—at the top.* Employers are no longer likely to write a letter, so it is more important to include a landline phone number, a cell number, and email. Remember, many employers are older people like myself and we still use email, even if many of our potential employees do not.[3] Similarly, it is important to continue checking one's email preferably twice a day as long as a job offer or further interview offer is still possible. Lack of a timely follow-up can lead to a missed job opportunity.

- *Clearly indicate experience and try to draw out experience which shows potential for doing the work that is advertised.* If the job is looking for someone with teamwork experience, then make sure to include examples of experience working with others. Again, this experience may have come from volunteering; however, it is still valuable and still needs to be written out on the resume, for example, "worked as part of a team of five who volunteered with Habitat for Humanity for one month."

---

3   My day-to-day experience working with students, together with research I have seen on the matter, suggests that today's students consider texting and tweeting the way to keep in touch. Employers are not yet likely to text a job offer or invitation for interview, so it is important to continue reading email.

or "Co-led a Sunday School class with three others, taking turns organizing portions of the daily lesson."

- *Place the category with the most relevant (to the job being applied for) experience closest to the top of the resume.* If a job description makes clear that the employer is looking for someone with teamwork experience, and the best example of teamwork experience is shown in one particular category, for example "Volunteer Work," then that is the category that should be placed up top. One may have had a part-time summer job that provided experience working with a diverse group of people; in that case the "Work Experience" category would belong near the top. Remember, it is less important what title the categories have and more important that they show the types of qualifications gained by different life experiences.

- *Mention any special skills or training.* Sub-headings could include "Certificates," "Achievements," "Honors and Awards," "Sports and Hobbies," "Special Interests," and "Languages Spoken." It is not necessary to use exactly the same category headers as others use, but again, limit categories to those things which are relevant on an entry-level resume. This is not the time to invent categories like, "Video Games" or "Favorite TV shows." Those who are multi-lingual should include the language(s) they speak on the resume, even if they are not directly related to the job—the ability to speak several languages indicates a person has experience with at least one other culture and most employers value this kind of experience.

- *What is decidedly not relevant?* Unless one is applying to test or design computer games, then one's gaming background is not only irrelevant, it could be problematic. I have a colleague who invited a real life employer into his classroom to talk to his students as they were working on resumes. One of the students said he was going to put his gaming experience on his resume because he thought it would be a cool fact that would make him stand out as an individual. The real life employer said, "Well, that's a resume I'd toss right in the garbage because I'd just figure you're going to goof off playing video games the minute my back's turned."

- *Facts that do not seem to offer anything to the employer are usually best left off a resume.* It is one thing to include "neutral" facts about hobbies and interests; it is advisable to check with several adults who are closer to the employer's age on the status of hobbies and interests if there is any doubt about their neutrality. Photography, skiing, hiking...okay... photographing vampires and Goths during the evenings (might raise concerns about an employee showing up tired from their wild night); skiing while pretending to be James Bond and wearing a tuxedo (might raise concerns the employee will be odd); hiking in preparation to head out to the North Pole during spring break (might raise concerns that this is an employee who is going to quit shortly after being trained); these are the kind of facts that while they might be true, are better left off a resume. A resume should be true but the truth needs to be targeted to someone who is going to entrust the person they hire with a business that is financially important.

- *A resume should show a person's potential to be someone worthy of trust.* The same is true for both part-time work and work study employment. On campus in a work study job, for instance, the adult staff who will supervise students tend to take their work very seriously, even if they do not "own" the company. They want to know that if they are going to be putting their time and energy into training a student, that student in turn is worth that time and energy; they are looking for students who will show up on time, pay attention to what they are told, and not be unpleasant to have in the work environment. It is just as important to be professional in a work study job as it is to be professional in a volunteer job.

Class Study Groups

Students at STEM schools seem to universally agree they do not like being forced to work with others on group projects in class—there are no guarantees that other students will work as hard as they do, or know as much as they do, and that is just one more person, or group of people, who have schedules that must be coordinated with. Ironically, it is impossible to get through a STEM education without doing class group work. In fact, group work is not only a fact of university life, it will often continue to be a fact of life for most of the graduates who leave school with a degree in a STEM field. Because the knowledge that is part of STEM fields is specialized knowledge, it is almost universally true that students will need to work with others in the contexts that their specialized knowledge will place them in. STEM fields include working with technicians, field assistants, managers, those one is responsible for supervising and possibly even students. These are groups of people with different levels of education, different backgrounds, different skills. They will know things that a specialist—which is what STEM education prepares one to be— does not know but needs to be aware of, or have skills that a team rely on to get their own work done. The sooner a person begins learning to co-operate with others—even if that has to begin with learning to tolerate being around others—the better.

Note to Students
To prepare for work in college:

- Start creating a resume while in high school.

- Continue to keep your resume updated as your knowledge and skills grow.

- Take time to target each version of your resume to the job you are applying for.

- Be prepared to cut/paste and have several versions of your resume as templates that you can adapt as necessary to new job opportunities.

Some families seem to imagine that because their child is very gifted in a specific area, for example math, that someone out in the world is going to pay their child to sit in a room by himself and conduct math experiments. I am not aware of this being true for anyone, anywhere. I am aware of an individual who had a great strength in cryptography who graduated from our university and was hired by the government and allowed to spend much of her time alone, breaking codes. Rumor has it she has even been provided with food and a bed in her work area. She still has to interact with others from time to time, in order to be given work assignments and to discuss the outcome of her work. I would imagine she is even required to attend some meetings where she is expected to communicate with others. My point is that, if a child is to grow up and survive outside their family's home as an independent adult, then he must learn to interact with others. And he is less likely to make it through even his freshman year of university if he has not practiced the ability to work with others in a group. Group work will be an ongoing feature of his life.

As I indicated in Chapter 2 when discussing children having personal aides in their primary and secondary education, and being excused from having to participate in group work, these accommodations cease to be aids at a certain point in a child's life. If a child has the intellectual capacity to attend a STEM university, then her family needs to be working with her on learning to work with others long before she arrives on a university campus. Remember, a student may be better served by taking at least a year to work as a volunteer in the community before moving on to university if she has not developed the capacity to work with others by the time she leaves high school.

Attempting to communicate with peers is probably the most challenging activity most of us in society take part in. Words are imprecise. People sometimes use a similar word to mean different things. Feelings and ideas are often hard to understand even when people are able and willing to discuss them. Children need a great deal of practice in peer relations and it may require an educational context to initially create these environments.

This is also where joining social groups as a family can be very helpful. Children can be provided with opportunities for meeting and interacting with others in a social area that is easier for them to tolerate. Sometimes communication can be facilitated by building communication around an activity that a child already enjoys. The more enjoyable they find an activity, the more likely a child is to want to communicate with others about this activity. Families will probably need to work closely with educators to discover how a child behaves with their peers outside of the home. Where are his strengths? Where does he need more practice? Is he easily engaged by other people's ideas, losing track of his independent thoughts? Is he reluctant to talk to anyone else? Does he need more practice sharing? Ask teachers not only where they witness a student's strengths but also where a student needs further social development; work with educators to ensure that a student is getting the right kinds of practice outside of school, which can reinforce what he is learning in school.

Families can allow children opportunities to conduct research and give presentations at home, particularly if the opportunity is not presented in school. A child learns more about expressing himself to peers, however, if he practices communicating in school as well as outside of school. Part of a child's educational experience should eventually include learning to communicate with others because this is a skill the child will continue to need throughout his life. A child may begin by needing reminders about talking to others in the way he would want to be talked to; he might need reminding to consider how he would talk if he knew a parent or teacher were standing over him listening. Children also need to learn to listen to others.

Listening is a skill that is every bit as difficult to learn as is speaking. For invisibly disabled children listening may be an even bigger challenge. They need practice. Listening is far too complex a skill for me to even consider covering in a few paragraphs here. If a young person finds it challenging to listen, including focusing for at least several minutes on what someone else is saying, then her family should seek out resources and educators who can assist in developing this practice. Communication, including listening, begins in large part with the ability to accept and work with those who are different from ourselves. An ability to tolerate others who may strike a young person as "boring" is another key to learning to listen. It may take the assistance of educators and communication experts to assist a child in learning to integrate these skills.

Remember, children will learn a great deal about accepting and co-operating with others by what they witness their parents doing. The example set by parents should also teach a child that we must all learn to work with people who may be different from us but who still have a place in our work and social world. If that is a lesson the parent still struggles with, then I strongly recommend that the family work together on practicing the skills related to taking turns sharing information. This is another example of where family meals can be useful, with each person practicing sharing and listening during the course of the meal. I've worked with some families where parents have found it helpful to enter therapy and work on their own challenges with communication, releasing control of growing children, and other personal struggles. When a child observes that their parent(s) are continuing to learn, it further reinforces the value of being open to new knowledge and experience. This is another important message for children to receive as they become adults— education and personal development are lifelong endeavors.

Professional and Social Groups

It should be noted that students will have organized opportunities for meeting other students who share their major, and theoretically at least some of their interests, once at university. Every field of study has at least one national/international professional organization that students can join; membership can be continued throughout one's professional career. This professional affiliation not only provides an important line on a student's curriculum vitae (which is what students get to call their resume if they obtain advanced degrees); membership also provides opportunities for networking. Once one enters a STEM field as a professional, one will start to meet other people working in the field at conferences and workshops, as well as on one's home campus. It is part of life in STEM fields that a student learns to start networking with other people doing similar work or research, including students who are attending different universities. Networking as a professional is necessary in part because it can lead to future research partnerships and research partnerships increase the probability of finding a funding agency which will financially support one's work—many STEM fields require professionals to seek out funding for their work. Even at universities, the university may only provide space for a professor to work in and the professor may need to seek out private and public funding to both equip their lab and pay for their research. This is also how many STEM jobs are funded for students—through research grants, awards, and contracts.

A student should begin practicing networking before she graduates from university. As a student one will find there are opportunities to work with professors and fellow students on shared research topics, poster presentations, and sometimes papers. Students who conduct research with professors will often then have the opportunity to attend a conference with the professor to present their work; many professors actively work with students to assist them with developing these kinds of professional experiences. These opportunities can be an important developmental step both personally and professionally. If one has any interest in graduate studies than experience with accompanying a professor to a conference is very important and can be gained by the senior year of one's undergraduate studies.

Regardless of whether or not a student intends to pursue graduate studies, meeting others in one's field of study/specialization can be an excellent way to develop friendships with people who share common interests, and can also be an important source of learning about employment opportunities, and gaining insider information about which employers are preferable and which less desirable. If, for example, I were to consider working at a different university, I know enough people in my specialized field of study that I can always find someone who has personal experience with a university that I would consider employment with. As a result, I can learn about the work environment, the way managers tend to treat employees, the types of work the department is specializing in, and the sort of local department politics that are part of every work environment. Some places are lovely to work for and others one would not wish on one's worst enemy. It can be very useful to have this type of information before accepting a job offer. Networking thus can have some very practical applications.

Friendships are also more naturally maintained when made with people who have common interests and the ability to discuss similar things. Ironically, as much as one's family may support one's study, the more specialized those studies become, the harder it will be to discuss what one does with anyone outside one's field of study. As a result, while one's family remains a constant support network it is one's colleagues who will share excitement and really "understand" when one makes important progress or has a significant lab result. Only another programmer is likely to truly appreciate the story of finding and rewriting the small bit of code that has caused a much larger system glitch, just as only another research chemist will really understand the nuances of a laboratory analysis of cigarette smoke.

The more specialized one's STEM field of study, the fewer the number of people who will understand one's work. Having friends and acquaintances within one's field significantly impacts a person's sense of wellbeing. It will be natural for these acquaintances and friendships to begin with those who share one's alma mater, that is, people who graduate from the same university.

Those who graduate from the same university—who share an alma mater—can also be very open to networking with others from "their school" regardless of how many years separate their actual graduation dates. Many universities offer alma mater gatherings for former graduates, not just on campus but also off-campus, around the nation, and in other countries. These gatherings are another opportunity for networking. It has been said that getting a job is only partially what one knows—it is also a matter of who one knows. Making personal connections with people in one's field of study and at least occasionally attending alma mater gatherings are further ways of connecting with people who may have valuable information or further connections that will aid one's career development.

Note to students

Meeting new people at social gatherings is one more skill that needs to be developed and many of us will find it is the skill we need the most practice with. Begin while in college. Join the professional group for your major and consider joining the honor society for your major—most fields have a specialized honor society. If you manage your time well you will also have opportunities to join clubs related to a hobby or sporting activity. Practicing social skills is an important part of the university experience. Having a social group on one's resume also can be the point that an interviewer latches onto and is able to talk to you about—remember, sometimes those conducting first-round interviews are in the human resource department—not STEM specialists.

7

Life isn't Fair and Other Truths

When I was in the sixth grade, attending a small, rural school, the highlight of the year for me was the visit of the Harlem Globetrotters basketball team. Our whole school was treated to a display of their skill and humor and I loved it.

A few weeks later, our English teacher assigned us an essay to be themed, "What I Want to do When I Grow Up."

My theme was about becoming a Harlem Globetrotter.

Even at that age the theme was written with a sense of bitter irony. Adults, particularly my teachers, were constantly telling me that with hard work I could grow up to be anything I wanted. As a white girl who was already topping out at my mature height of 5'4" (162.5cm). I knew perfectly well I could not be a Harlem Globetrotter—but that seemed like the ideal job and lifestyle to me. I was stuck between wanting someone to be more honest with me about my real possibilities and frustrated by people like my maternal grandmother who insisted my real possibilities were limited to nurse or receptionist (she thought my struggles in school precluded me from choosing the career she had—elementary school teacher).

Adults are particularly fond of telling young people the partial truth that a child can "grow up to be anyone" (i.e. any social position/ career). Of course this is not true. The partial truth contained in this statement is that a child's limits are yet to be discovered. With a combination of education, rehabilitation, encouragement, and opportunities to practice new skills children can reach goals that might initially seem impossible. I am living proof of that. We can choose to help our children, teaching and encouraging them to constantly develop their potential. As young people with disabilities, we can choose to work hard or choose to sit back and complain about the overwhelming unfairness of life. We can even be like the parents in Chapter 2 who sat back and prayed for a miracle, refusing to help their son learn even basic skills. If you are reading this then you obviously are hoping to assist your child or yourself reach the greatest possible potential. You are willing to put time, effort, education, and preparation into a goal. Working hard is not enough to overcome all obstacles though. A disability cannot be wished away or worked away, or accommodated away. While our limits are unknown our disabilities do impose some restrictions.

I vividly remember when I was young watching a news report about a man who wanted to be a mounted police officer—the kind that ride a horse patrolling the streets and are so helpful with crowd control. This man was living with a form of dwarfism. The police department had a policy that in order to be a mounted police officer a candidate needed to be able to mount and dismount the horse without aid. I remember watching this man on television as he tried to jump up and grab the saddle. He could only reach the stirrup and did not have sufficient upper body strength to pull himself up from there to the horse's back.

Sometimes when an individual has an invisible disability either they or their family seem to lose sight of the fact, at least from time to time, that invisible disabilities create physical realities, just as visible disabilities do—the difference is that because the disability cannot be "seen" it is not as clear what those limitations will be. One might be able to look at a person in a wheelchair and quickly realize they cannot walk; it is much harder for people to understand the physical limitations imposed by dyslexia because these limitations cannot be seen (this is true for all invisible disabilities and the physical limitations, or brain differences, which cause them). How quickly and efficiently a person with dyslexia can learn to read will vary from individual to individual—no dyslexic individual, however, has the physical capacity to learn/process language as quickly as one of their peers who has no language processing disorder; if they are given the same amount of time and the same resources the person with dyslexia will be "behind" their non-disabled peers. This is no more a lack of effort than is using a wheelchair rather than walking due to a physical disability. The lack of ability has nothing to do with willingness or effort—the lack of ability is directly related to physical limitations.

It seems to me that life presents us with challenges, some we can overcome and some are beyond what our physical and emotional make-up will allow us to achieve. Each individual will have to recognize what is a challenging but attainable goal for him or herself. Refusing to accept the physical realities of our disabilities, however, places us in a position of great frustration and ongoing defeat. I believe in setting personal goals that at least occasionally allow for success.

Difficult versus Impossible

I was able to struggle through math until I arrived in my junior year of high school. Then it was like my brain hit a wall. Even with tutoring, time with teachers, and repeating the class, I could not hold the formulas in my head and see how to apply the same formula to different sets of numbers. I remember one tutor trying to assist me by pointing out, "You use the same formula on this problem that you just used on the last problem." This was no more helpful to me then when my first grade teacher had said, "This is a letter, this is a number!" as if that information by itself was supposed to "educate" me about something. After two attempts at Algebra, I had two credits for Business Math—two different teachers felt so sorry for me after watching me struggle in the class that they could not fail me and instead they gave me credit for what was considered a "lower" form of math. I found this ironic since I understood even less about Business Math than I did about Algebra; I did, however, appreciate being given credit for my effort.

For whatever reason my brain processes information the way it does, there are some things that are very difficult for me to learn and some things that are closer to impossible. I believe this is true for many people—we have things we do well and things we struggle with. The amount of time and effort I have to put into getting anything out of Algebra showed me that this was not my strength in life. I could have chosen to continue to struggle with Algebra but even with years of time and effort, even if I had scraped through and managed to get a degree in mathematics, why would anyone hire me in this subject area, or provide a graduate education for me in this subject area when there are so many better qualified people who do not have to struggle so much to learn so little? I often tell young people, education is supposed to be challenging—it is not supposed to be painful. While an individual *can choose* to set a goal that may be impossible, or nearly impossible to reach, I encourage people to *set goals that while challenging are obtainable.* It seems to me that living with one or more invisible disabilities provides enough challenges in life; we do not have to add to our personal misery and anxiety by setting our sights on goals that are in direct conflict with our disabilities.

I do believe in hard work; I am dyslexic and have degrees in writing and communication. That wasn't easy. It was, however, manageable because once I learned to read I found I loved it. Once I learned about communication I found writing a great way to share my ideas with other people and while regularly frustrated and challenged, I wanted to improve my writing ability. While I had to work very, very hard I knew that my goal to improve my writing was not beyond my reach—it was something I would have to stretch myself to obtain though. It is a very real challenge helping a child recognize the difference between working on a goal that is very challenging and one that is impossible. It may take some trial and error to discover the right career path. Life is unfair, so sometimes we will really want something, work hard towards it, and we will not be particularly successful. I suggest that a young person ask herself, "Do I want this degree so badly that the struggle to get through the classes I need to obtain the degree is worth it to me?" If the destination you have set for yourself isn't worth the road you have to travel to reach it, then it may be that the destination needs to change—don't expect the road to magically morph into a more desirable one.

How to Choose a Career

It is important to know the difference between the hobbies one enjoys and the skills and capacities one has that facilitate employability. This may sound like the exact opposite advice that career counselors might give, "Find a hobby you like and see if there is a way to make that into a full-time job." Let me explain why I am taking a different track than a career counselor might. Many, many people enjoy video games, or shopping, or talking on the phone. Very, very few people have the collection of skills and abilities and personality that will suit them to being a video game designer or tester, a personal shopper, or a phone representative (most likely sales representative) for a company.

I will use the example of a video game designer: it is not enough to love gaming. One has to be able to spend long hours working alone writing very exacting code on a computer—the attention to detail needed is extremely high as computer code does not work unless it is exactly correct—there is no room for error. When one isn't working alone for long hours, one has to be able to successfully meet with the team of developers who are also working on the game. One has to be able to communicate clearly with others, respond in a timely manner to requests for information that may interrupt the actual code-writing for the game; one has to be able to work with others and alone almost equally well. This is not a common set of skills. Many people can write code, or work with others, far fewer can do both.

Making Career Choices

It can be useful for the student to talk to a career counselor. This is not the same as a school guidance counselor—career counselors specialize in helping people find the most appropriate fields of study and work.

A career counselor will make use of computer programs and tests that explore a person's strengths, interests, and aptitudes, as well as her dislikes and limitations. When speaking to the career counselor it is important to be just as honest about one's weaknesses as one's strengths; being brilliant at computers but disliking working in groups of people is the sort of information a career counselor needs to accurately guide a student towards an appropriate field of study.

It is also sensible to talk to at least two people who are already doing the job. Sometimes a job sounds good—perhaps there are a number of openings and the pay scale is impressive. This is limited information and there may be details about actually performing a job which make the work difficult or unattractive to some people. Not everyone would make a good dentist, no matter how much demand and how good the salary for this work. When possible a student should try and arrange to job-shadow a professional in the field he is interested in. This is an opportunity that a career counselor at school may be able to assist in arranging. Job-shadowing, or at least being introduced to someone already working in a field is also a perfect opportunity to learn more about both the work environment and the educational challenges of preparing for a career in the field.

If a student is given an opportunity to meet a professional working in the field she aspires to, one of the questions to ask is, "What were the challenges in getting this degree?" This is also an opportunity to inquire about the day-to-day challenges of carrying out the job. There are several other questions that one should ask of people already working in the field:

- What are the best schools to attend for this major?

- What were the job placement rates[1] when you graduated?

- How many months did it take you to find work?

It may also be possible for a student to volunteer to work with someone who is working in the field the student thinks he wants to major in. A successful job-shadowing experience may be a natural lead-in to asking about volunteering with a professional. Pre-veterinarian students will often begin by volunteering one afternoon a week in a local vet clinic to gain experience; some will then find this leads to part-time employment once they begin university.

How to Choose a College

Once a student has identified an area of work/career field she believes would be a good fit for herself, given what her strengths and limits are, she should begin to look for a STEM university that is known for graduating students in this field; again, this is where having talked to people already working in the field will be helpful. Most people know which schools are best known for graduating students in their area of specialization. A student may start by attending a local community college before moving on to the STEM university that she will eventually graduate from—she will still want a fair idea of the STEM university she eventually plans to apply to. The classes taken at community college will ideally apply towards a final degree,

---

1   The job placement rate refers to the percentage of students who graduate with a degree and then go on to find work; the higher the placement rate, the more people who graduated and were able to go on to work or further study.

which means knowing what the degree requirements are at the university one is aiming for. A student and his family should begin by looking for colleges that have a reputation for producing graduates who work in the desired career field. A school may have an overall good or average reputation, yet one department might be very well known and regarded—or have a rather poor reputation. The school's and department's reputations are only part of what a student should consider; the student also needs to consider the placement rate for graduates from the specific department he will be studying with—if a department is not placing their graduated students in paid positions, then the degree a student is working for might be considered to be of rather limited value. Read the online school catalogue to see which classes are needed in order to obtain a degree in the field; schools have different requirements for similar degrees so a student and his family should never assume that all schools will expect the same thing from a student.

Students should also seek out online chat rooms where current students are discussing their experiences with classes and professors at each specific school the student is considering. At any given point in time, a school may have a particular department that is difficult to work with or a professor who is particularly inspirational. If students are complaining of a department or class, be aware of this before a student is committed to a course of study that will place this department/class directly in her path—there is always more than one school/department that a student can study with, even if a different school is not the student's first choice.

I would suggest it is also increasingly important for students in general, and invisibly disabled students in particular, to look for a school with a strong track record of getting their students internships or co-ops before the students graduate. Consider that each year a number of people with the exact same degree graduate from each school. What causes one potential employee to stand out from others to an employer are the actual incidents of previous similar employment the person is offering. Why hire someone who has a degree alone, when another individual has both the degree and has spent a summer doing a very similar kind of work to that being hired for? Co-ops and internships also frequently create openings for further work with the same company once a student graduates with her degree.

For some students international study is important either for their personal or professional goals; once again, look for a school with an already developed international program of study in the country that the student wishes to study in; if a student struggles to learn languages then he will benefit from attending a school that offers study abroad in countries which speak his native language.

Note to students
Before committing to a school:

- Make sure to visit the campus.

- If possible, sit in on a class that you would eventually need to take.

- Talk to other students about their experience and what they like and dislike about their courses and campus.

- Talk to the disability service provider on campus to ensure that receiving accommodations will not be difficult (and also to determine how comfortable you are with the person or people in this office since they should be able to act as an academic support for you).

The Unfairness—and Reality— of Mandatory Classes

For those familiar with dyslexia or who have read this book from the beginning to this point, it will come as no great surprise that as someone living with dyslexia I struggle with learning other languages; I struggled to learn to read and write English and there are days when I still feel like it is a second language to me. It was beyond frustrating for me to discover that I could not obtain a graduate degree without the necessity of having to struggle with mandated classes in other languages and classes in formal logic—formal logic requires the ability to put words into formulas and work through the formulas to achieve a result. As someone who struggles with formulas this also seemed unfair—particularly given that my areas of interest had nothing to do with translating from other languages or carrying out formal logic.

I had such difficulty with these expectations that they did by necessity influence the graduate schools I applied to. Once I had a list of all possible graduate schools, I had to remove from that list schools which required me to be able to read/write/test in *two* additional languages. I knew I would struggle meeting a single language requirement. I also removed schools that required more than one formal logic class. From that reduced list I looked for schools and programs that would allow me to primarily focus on classes that I could manage with hard work, against schools that would require too many classes that I knew I would struggle with no matter how much time and energy I put into those classes.

Not all mandatory classes will seem fair or make sense. Some requirements are left-overs from an age when research included being able to read primary texts in the original languages they were written in. Requirements have not necessarily changed to reflect that much research is now written in English. If a class is required in order to obtain a degree, do not expect an accommodation that will excuse a student from the class.

Another important note: do not take word of mouth as proof that an exemption will be allowed for anyone. *If an agreement between the student and the school is not in writing no exemption can be guaranteed.* In other words, if someone at the school verbally assures a student or her family that she will be exempted from a course normally required for the degree, this agreement needs to be in writing, and it needs to be approved by both the Chair of the Department granting the degree, and by the Registrar's office.

Always review the course catalogue (mainly online now) for the specific degree requirements needed to graduate. Remember, though, that catalogues and requirements change from year to year—a student will be responsible for meeting the requirements of the catalogue in effect the year she entered the university. If there are questions about this, the academic advisor for the major can help a student clarify what she needs to do—what classes she needs to take and any additional requirements she needs to meet (such as writing a certifying test for her field.) If a student, at any point in her university career, does not understand what is required of her, she should contact the academic advisor for her department.

I recently worked with a young man who is dyslexic, has difficulty memorizing, and is gifted at math. His mother wanted reassurance that once he began his studies in the Math Department at our university, his ability to work mathematical formulas would be what counted, not his inability to hold large formulas in his memory. I told her I simply could not give her this guarantee; she and her son needed to speak directly with the Chair of the Math Department to discover what would be considered "necessary knowledge/skills" in order for the student to graduate. This meeting led to a very productive conversation and the young man was given clear assurances and explanations of what would and would not be necessary in order for him to obtain his degree. Just as importantly, I think, he became a person that the Chair was personally interested in, and set himself apart from other entering freshmen students as a student who was willing to go to some personal effort to reach his goals. These kinds of personal connections and demonstrations of interest are the kind of qualities that assist a student in being successful and help him to stand out in a positive way to his department.

Choosing your School = "More Fairness"

I initially attended a local community college for one semester after high school. I was not ready to be back in school and that school and I were not a good fit. I left after one semester with credit for three classes and a 2 GPA. I did not go back to school for about eight years. When I decided that I was ready to try again, I applied to the university that was nearest where my parents were living. Those three classes from years ago actually qualified me as a "transfer" student and I was given rather quick acceptance, despite my rather humble GPA.

I believe people should seriously consider the value of local community colleges as a place to start their education, particularly if none of their first choices for a STEM university accept them in their first round of applications. Once a student has even a semester of community college he is no longer applying as an entering freshman, but rather he is considered a transfer student. I was a bit of an anomaly as I did much better once in university than I had in community college; most people can use community college as a place to improve their grades. Starting at a local community college can also help a student make a smoother transition from home to independent life.

I frequently find myself advising students who have come directly from home to this school to withdraw for at least one semester, and attend a community college closer to their home, family, and familiar support network.

College Applications

Some people will send out 15 or 20 applications to universities. I fail to see the value of this method. I believe in being realistic but selective. If a student's only choices are schools with highly competitive entrance requirements, then the student may not be accepted in his first round of applications. If, however, a student selectively aims his applications at schools that have entrance requirements he clearly meets and even exceeds, then he should not require more than five or six applications to be offered a seat in at least one program. And if I'm wrong, and a student is not accepted to his first five or six *reasonable* choices, then I would suggest his application may not be as strong as he believes it to be, and he might be best served by spending at least one semester in community college strengthing his resume, by which I mean achieving better grades and more social practice.

Every semester I will encounter a family whose son or daughter has accepted entrance to our university while holding the misguided understanding that because their student was given a certain type of accommodation in their previous education they will be allowed this accommodation in university. For a more in-depth discussion of how accommodation and legal requirements change upon entering college please see Chapter 2. At this point it might help if I briefly review how a university sets the standards a student must meet in order to obtain a degree.

Universities are divided into departments under the different fields of study. For example, my PhD came from the Humanities Department, which was within the Arts and Sciences field at the university I graduated from. In order to obtain my degree there were a set number of classes I had to take—my mandatory classes. There were also a set number of classes I had to take where I was allowed to select classes from a list of qualifying classes. To obtain a degree every student will have to take some mandatory classes, and will be able to choose some classes from a list of classes that meet the requirements of the degree they are seeking. Some programs of study will allow for more choices than others—I understand that currently the engineering students at our university have five or fewer choices they get to make while the bulk of their studies are set out in a year-by-year lock-step fashion for them.

Note to Students
Choosing where to apply

- Review the online catalogue of required classes for any school and degree you are interested in.

- Short-list those schools which have a list of classes that you are confident you can be successful in (you can find course descriptions for each offered class also in the online course catalogue.)

- If you struggle with a particular type of learning, for example languages, look for schools that allow for options such as learning Sign Language as opposed to a spoken language, that allow for a year of study of a subject versus a one-time test, or that will modify expectations to accommodate you.

- *Know before you go*—do not assume that because of your disability you will be allowed an exemption from an arcane degree requirement to obtain your degree.

The unfairness of choice or lack of choice

No matter how a student's course of study is set up—with a great deal of choice or with almost no choice—the system will be unfair for someone. Students who like choices might chafe under a lock-step program that an engineering degree generally requires, while students in a program like general biology might be annoyed that there are multiple choices, perhaps none of them actually appealing to the student. I have often heard the complaint that a department never seems to offer the one class "everyone really wants to take" and instead "only offers classes the professors are interested in teaching." I would suggest a student's first clue that she may be in the wrong field of study should be a lack of interest in what the professors are generally teaching...

University does not allow an undergraduate student to design their own course of study. Application to university means a student is asking to be given professional qualifications in a specific field. The student does not determine what the requirements of the field are; the student is required to meet the expectations of the field. If a student proves unable to meet these expectations, then those who are the authorities in the field will say the student has failed to qualify; they do not consider the field itself "fair" or "unfair." They consider the individual either qualified or unqualified. Again, unlike earlier educational contexts, there is no expectation that a university will teach everyone who is interested in a particular field of study. A student's application will be considered and even if he is granted permission to take classes, a student can be required to leave classes by the university, dismissed from his course of study, or told that he is not fit for the field he initially entered in and must choose a different course of study. Allow me to explain:

- Students must take the requisite classes to earn a degree.

- Each student must maintain a grade point average (GPA) set by the department and by the school.

- Failure to maintain the required GPA can mean dismissal.

- Failure to maintain a department's GPA in the classes that count towards the student's major (e.g. chemistry, computers, communication) can mean dismissal from a field of study.

- Once a department has dismissed a student, the student will either have to find a new field of study or leave the university.

One final note about required classes—not all of them will be academic or in a student's specialized area of interest. Most schools require students to take several credits of physical education—this can be anything from bowling to rowing and varies from school to school. Most schools will require everyone to take at least some classes from the following list:

- math

- reading/writing

- philosophy/sociology/anthropology

- science with a laboratory section

- physical education.

Again, it does not matter what a student's major is. Every school has requirements that are considered "general education"—in other words, that are designed to help a student be more well-rounded in her education. If a student does not wish to study anything aside from hands-on application, then the student should be investigating technical colleges, not STEM universities. Technical colleges allow for the direct application of basically everything a student is required to learn in class.

It is important to point out that not everyone will be happy pursuing a professional degree in a STEM university, even if initially this seems like an appropriate choice. Technical colleges and degrees are very valuable and employable at this point in time. If a student finds herself with a specific interest and does not desire a professional degree to be personally satisfied, then I would be hard pressed to suggest why she should pursue a professional education over a technical one.

The Difference between Unfair and Potentially Illegal

"This assignment isn't fair," the young man complained. He'd waited after class to tell me this, although he had not managed to arrive on time to class.

I replied, "As I've said from the beginning of the semester, this class is designed to replicate the kind of environment you will face in real life when you go to work. Work isn't fair."

"But I hate group work! I should be able to work alone."

"When you graduate will you be starting your own company, with your own money and no other employees?"

"No."

I nodded. "That means you will be working with others. This class is designed to give you practice working with others."

The student's email was specific and to the point.

On x day, in x class, the teacher had given her a test but refused to allow her the extended time that was part of her accommodation. I immediately contacted the responsible faculty member and asked him if he wanted me to give the student her make-up test in my office.

The faculty member's response: "It was just a quiz and she did fine."

My reply basically clarified that any timed and graded assignment that was given in a class had to be given with extended time; the student could choose to forgo her make-up test if she was satisfied with her grade; however, she was entitled to a make-up test if she wanted one.

In the first scenario, I annoyed a student—as I often do—by having a standard set of expectations that everyone finds annoying. All the students in class tend to groan when I announce that, in a class focused on teaching students real-world technical communication procedures, they will have to work with other people, that is "group work." STEM fields require the ability to work with others, therefore everyone in my classes is required to practice working with others. Students have yet to be delighted when I announce this at the beginning of the semester, yet this is not an illegal practice, even if I am subjecting a disabled student to group work he finds distasteful.

In the second scenario a teacher—I believe in this case unintentionally—violated a student's legal rights by refusing to give this student her accommodations. This was incorrect on the faculty member's part; by allowing the student the option to write a new, equivalent quiz (an option she ultimately turned down when she discovered she had received a good grade on the quiz she had already taken) we managed to avoid actually breaking the law. Legally, a university is usually allowed to "make up" a mistake before a student is in a position to sue the school for violating her rights to a fair education.

How then, does a student know the difference between events on campus that are just annoying and events that are potentially illegal? Who can a student turn to for assistance when she is uncomfortable with something that happened at college? Consider the following guidelines when deciding if a teacher's assignment, expectation, or behavior is just annoying or potentially illegal.

In the case of a *universal class expectation* (meaning that everyone in class has to do an activity or assignment) if the student believes his accommodation would alter this expectation in his case:

1. First try to discuss changes to the assignment with the professor in case independent negotiation is possible.

2. If a solution cannot be reached between the student and the teacher, then the disability service provider can meet with both the professor and the student to help negotiate or alter the expectation.

In the case of a *limited class expectation* (meaning that some students are given one kind of assignment and others are given a different assignment, or students are assigned specific tasks as part of a group assignment) if a student feels her assignment is in conflict with her disability:

1. Approach the instructor during his/her office hours; explain how the task is complicated by the disability; work with the professor to modify the assignment.

2. If the professor will not work with the student, then the student should contact the disability service provider and request assistance.

If a student is concerned that *a professor seems to be grading him unfairly*, or is showing some prejudice towards him due to his disability:

1. At the university level it is always expected that a student will *first* discuss concerns with the professor.

2. If the student remains unsatisfied or is afraid to talk directly to the professor, the next step is to talk to the Chair of the Department.

3. If the student is not satisfied by a discussion with the Department Chair the next step is to speak with the Ombudsperson for the university.

4. If the university has no Ombudsperson, then the student should make an appointment to speak to someone in the Dean of Students' or Chancellor's office.

If a professor is requiring a student do something that no one else in the class is required to do, meaning that *the expectation is unique to that one student* in a class:

1. The student should first discuss this with the professor and see if there is a reason for this—it may be that the professor is trying to accommodate the student and whether the accommodation is working or not, the initial discussion should be between professor and student.

2. If the student is uncomfortable at this point talking to the professor, then she should seek out her academic advisor and clarify if the professor's expectation is reasonable for the field of study she is in.

3. If the student is not satisfied with the academic advisor's response, then the student should speak to the Chair of the Department.

The proper chain of command in university for resolving a conflict

There are a series of steps a student is expected to follow when the student has a complaint about a teacher. *The first step is always to talk to the professor.* Always first allow for a direct resolution of the problem (students who skip this step will almost always be sent back to try talking to their professor before anyone else will work with them). Note: the exception to the rule of talking to a teacher directly is when the teacher has done or said something which makes a student uncomfortable enough that he feels physically, academically, or emotionally threatened. On the other hand, if a student has great difficulty speaking with professors he can ask either his academic advisor or disability service provider to accompany him to a meeting as his support person; the student should still speak for himself and not expect his advisor to negotiate for him.

If a student is not satisfied with the results of meeting directly with a professor, the next step in the university process is to speak with the Department Chair. The final person one can appeal to is the Ombudsperson; if there is no Ombudsperson, then make an appointment to meet with the Dean of Students or Chancellor.

Note to Students

If a teacher is making you very uncomfortable, the first person to speak to is the Chair of the Department in which the professor teaches. If a fellow student is making you very uncomfortable *in class*, then the teacher of the class is the first person to speak to. If a fellow student is making you very uncomfortable *outside of class*, then the first person to speak to is the staff member in charge of student conduct—every campus has such a person and if you cannot locate their office through an online search or the campus directory, then call the Dean of Students'/Chancellor's office and ask who/where this person is.

When a student is uncertain where else to turn, she can always begin by asking the disability service provider for advice. This office and the people in it are not limited to making sure a student receives her accommodation, this office can also help students negotiate the university system by assisting in identifying who to speak to and where to find key personnel. I regularly answer questions for students regarding who they should talk to for situations ranging from how to get yogurt in the morning (speak to dining services) to where to register for classes (usually online.)

The Dean of Students, or Chancellor, also has a mission to assist students in being successful in university. Again, this office should not be the first stop for students or families with questions—there are many other people on campus who answer questions and they can be found listed in a campus directory and online. Sometimes a student or parent will feel like they are "getting the runaround" or they will have a question other people are unable to answer; this is when it is time to make an inquiry at the Dean or Chancellor's office. Remember, however, that speaking to someone *in* the Dean or Chancellor's office is not the same as needing to speak *to* the Dean or Chancellor in person. The staff surrounding the Dean/Chancellor can answer basically every university-related question a student or his family will have. It is not necessary to call, or walk into the office, and insist on seeing the Dean/Chancellor in person. The member of staff who hears the question or concern will tell people if their need requires a personal meeting with someone else and will assist in making an appointment for a meeting. The Dean/Chancellor is very busy with administrative matters and, as a result, tends to be surrounded by staff who are very well versed in answering university-related questions. Memebers of staff also have jobs that are directly related to providing services which students and families are contacting the office for information about. For example, students and families often call the Dean of Students' office and say they *need* to talk to the Dean, when in reality they need to speak with me in my capacity as the Coordinator of Student Disability Services. This is just a reminder that sometimes the best thing to do is contact the Dean's office and state the reason for the call so that the member of staff can best direct the enquiry.

8

When a Parent Should be Involved

The Dean of Students sat in my office, my office phone was set to "speaker" and it sat between us. When the parent on the other end of the line answered, the Dean introduced herself and me. She explained the purpose of our call: the parent's son was someone we were very concerned about due to his emotional struggles and disruptive behavior. Then the Dean paused and allowed what she had said to sink in. A moment of silence was followed by one question from the parent.

"Well, what do you expect me to do about it?"

Our eyes widened as the Dean and I exchanged a surprised look. It is common for parents to try and manage their child's life from a distance and we are used to getting phone calls where parents try and give us explicit instructions regarding their opinion of what we should be doing for their child. This parent seemed to be at the other end of the spectrum, completely uninvolved in the outcome of their child's fate.

I said, "The first thing we'd like you to do is reach out to your son. Can you call him and ask him how he is? Try offering to speak with him about his struggles."

There was another pause. "I'll have to call my spouse at work," the parent finally replied. "This is a lot to take in and I really don't know what we can do about it."

When the parent had hung up I had to remind the Dean and myself, "Sometimes when a student has a lot of trouble functioning it is because their parents had trouble functioning and the student has never seen good problem-solving modeled...I hope the other parent in this family is a problem-solver."

Reasons for "The Call"

As explained in Chapter 2, federal law and privacy rights keep a university from freely sharing information about a student with their family. Unlike high school, where the principal might immediately contact parents with concerns, in university when the administrator reaches the point of calling a parent, it is typically a last resort, with other methods of intervention and assisting a student having not produced sufficient results.

Universities treat students as adults. When administrators call from university to express concern, they are usually at the point where they believe that a student has become a threat to himself or possibly others. The administration is contacting parents so that they can immediately intervene in their child's welfare. This may begin with a phone call but will almost always require a parent to make a personal trip to the school. Families may need to assist their student in seeking immediate medical treatment for depression, suicidal thoughts, or anger. Families may need to personally assess with the institution if it is feasible for the student to complete his semester of study, or if he needs to withdraw and go home, or into a hospital or treatment center.

The other reason a family is most likely to be called by their student but with a school administrator also in the room or participating in a conference call, is when the student has broken a conduct rule. By the time administrators offer to be in the room while a student calls home, she has probably incurred a financial penalty or is being charged with a crime. In "smaller" incidents of conduct violations the school does not tend to recommend that a student contact her parents. When the student, however, faces criminal charges, or incurs a large fine, then generally administrators will encourage the student to share this information with their parents so that they have some emotional and perhaps financial support in getting through the processes that the student faces. The university administration may also be requiring the student to leave school for suspension if the conduct they violated includes threatening behavior or academic misconduct.

Occasionally, university administration needs to encourage students to call their parents to inform them that the student needs to go home and is literally being barred from campus property. There have been incidents where a student's behavior has threatened others' wellbeing and, as a result, the university has required the student to immediately leave campus; where I work we have even put a student in a motel room and made sure his parents were informed by the student that the student was not being allowed to return to campus for a set period of time. At that point, a family generally needs to pick their student up immediately, or start paying to keep their student in a motel for a lengthy period of time—during which he may be getting into further trouble in town.

Note: when I say a student's behavior has "threatened others" please do not immediately think of the most extreme cases, where a student is threatening large numbers of anonymous people. Sometimes a student will have a very violent disagreement with *one other student* and based on the nature of the threats or interactions between these two students, either or both students may be suspended and barred from campus. If the school is concerned that a student could do serious harm to another, specific person on campus due to actions she has already taken, then the student could be suspended and barred from campus property. On our campus we have had to occasionally assist one student in obtaining a protection order against another student; in such cases the student who has the order against him is not able to be within a set distance of the other student. Violation of the protection order can also lead to suspension and being physically barred from campus property.

Students can also violate university policies while off campus. Off-campus behavior that leads to criminal charges will usually result in campus-conduct charges: facilitating drinking amongst minors; using drugs; impaired driving; theft; vandalism...if a student is in this kind of trouble off campus it will almost always have repercussions for him on campus.

Note to Students

Having to be in court, or being held in jail is not recognized as an "excused absence" at university. It is seen as a student choosing to behave in ways that have very real consequences for him, including negatively impacting his grade through missed work and being absent. Similarly, telling a teacher you were too drunk to do your homework, or too hungover to come to class will not only fail to win a student sympathy, it will certainly not improve the teacher's impression of the student. We expect the students we accept to university to be serious about the academic commitment required to be here. Allowing social, recreational, or other events to interfere with academics are seen as examples of a student making poor choices.

The Importance of Class Attendance

The student looked at his feet as he explained the reason he needed to miss school for several days. "My parents divorced and my dad was moving out. He told me to come home and help him."

While we had a great deal of sympathy for this student and his family situation—not to mention compassion for the extremely poor judgment his father had shown in making this demand—we were not able to give the student an "excused absence" from classes. He had unfortunately missed classwork and he would be penalized for this; his father's choice would negatively impact the son's grade. This may seem unduly harsh. The reality is that universities cannot attempt to judge how serious or important social and family events are to individual families. We have standard policies in place so that all students have equal treatment. If a parent or sibling dies, a student is generally excused from missing several days of class. If the student is in an accident and requires medical treatment, they are excused from class; it is always still up to the student to make up missed work as best they can, and possibly have a lower grade because their work cannot be fully made up.

Student Illness

Virtually every student gets sick during their first semester of college. Viruses, stomach flu, cold, strep throat, sinus infection—these are all more likely when someone is under stress, their eating and sleeping patterns have changed, and they are suddenly responsible for self-care on a level they've never been before. Add this to the fact they are living with a population of hundreds of other people in the same boat and you basically have a very productive germ and infection factory. Several things can be very helpful to a student when she gets sick away from home, her own room, and her family:

- A survival kit for cold and flu: throat lozenges, cough medicine, pain/fever relief tablets, over-the-counter medicine for upset stomach, facial tissues, lip balm.

- A care package from home: getting a card with a note, some soup and cookies or other edibles can do wonders to lift spirits, which aids recovery.

- A reminder to the student when it is time for them to go to a health clinic. If symptoms are persisting, then they may need medicine—if a student is missing classes then medical documentation from a doctor, clinic, or hospital will allow a student to make up at least some of her missed work.

Students may also need reminders to email their professors and be in touch about missed work—and then making up the work they missed due to illness. If a student struggles with organization, a parent could help them make a list of the assignments they've missed due to illness. They may also need assistance with carrying out a specific plan for catching up in class; if a family is not able to assist with this planning they can encourage a student to talk to an academic advisor.

It can also be helpful to remind a student of the different types of academic support on campus that can also assist them with homework. Many learning centers allow students to do homework in the center and ask questions when they encounter a difficulty—if this isn't possible, then it should be possible to make an appointment with a tutor in the learning center to work one-on-one over homework. Students can quickly become overwhelmed after an illness when they need to catch up on missed work; families are a good resource for reminding students of their options. It is also helpful for families and students to understand that missing too much class due to illness is usually a valid reason for the student to drop a class—or a semester—

rather than have the professors provide "make-up" work. The thinking at the university level is that if a student needs to miss too many classes, no matter how valid their reason—including ongoing injuries and need for medical treatment—then the student is best served by withdrawing for the remainder of the semester. Anything that keeps a student from class for a long enough period of time that it will impact their schoolwork, is keeping them from learning the material they are expected to know when they finish the class. Therefore, if a student has to miss a significant number of classes they should either drop the class, or withdraw from the university for the remainder of the semester.

In high school the knowledge a child is expected to acquire is often spread over a large period of an academic year. College courses are designed to run on a much tighter timeline. Depending on whether a university is on a quarterly or semester basis, students will have about 7 to 14 weeks in which they are expected to learn and complete assignments well enough to earn a good grade. In that time frame there will be reading, quizzes, tests, perhaps a presentation, group project, mid-term and end-of-term exams. This same rapid pace must be kept up in three to six classes at a time. A student really cannot academically afford to miss classes. Potential absences should be reserved for when the student is too sick to go to class. When I teach I will tell students, "You are allowed to miss two classes—for any reason. Save these absences for illness, weddings, funerals, court dates, and accidents. If you miss any further classes than two, these absences will decrease your grade…missing several classes will thus lower your grade in this class an entire level, from an A to an A- or a B- to a C+."

Of course, it never fails that a student in a class that I have told this to will then do all their work well but miss more classes than they are allowed; the smart ones realize to expect a final grade lower than an A. The grading policy I use is in the syllabus I give out at the beginning of the semester. I repeat all this information in class. I tend not to have a great deal of sympathy for students who do not take this message seriously because part of what I am grading on is the ability of a student to show up and work each class—again we are practicing real world skills the students will need when trying to hold a job. Employers typically take a dim view of workers who periodically just fail to show up to work be it because they wanted a day off or because they were taking a vacation with their family and did not make arrangements for this vacation not to impact their other obligations. Parents can assist their children by reinforcing the message that class is not to be missed unless one is simply too ill to attend. Professionals are allowed sick days—they are also expected to inform their employer that they will not be into work due to illness. I expect this from students in classes I teach as well. Like many professors, I expect students to be starting to develop the professionalism they will need to maintain their careers.

Documentation

It has been commented that nothing is as fatal to the health of grandparents as having a grandchild enter university. This tongue-in-cheek remark comes from the observation by faculty and administrators that one of the most common reasons given by students for needing to miss class is that one of their grandparents has died. Some students claim to lose a grandparent each semester they are in university.

Students and their families should thus not be surprised or offended when a student is required to show an obituary or funeral program to university officials or a professor to document a funeral. In order to maintain a standard and policy, universities usually require documentation of every funeral, accident and death that a student misses school for, if the student wants leeway in making up missed work.

- Check the university's online attendance policy.

- Be prepared with documentation of why classes were missed—funeral program, form from doctor, accident report from police.

- Bring documentation to the Dean or Chancellor's office if the university's policy allows for verified absences from school.

Note to Parents
Family Events

- Families can assist their students by not planning important family events to occur during the course of a semester. Consult the online school calendar for scheduled breaks and holidays.

- Schedule important events like family reunions, vacations, and weddings during breaks when the student will have enough time not only to be there but also to travel to the destination and return to school on time.

- Recognize that if a family member dies during the semester, a child in university may have to miss attending the funeral—a memorial service or gathering can be held which includes the student during their next visit home.

- This isn't high school—missing class time cannot be made up by doing homework while away.

- Some professors count attendance and participation as part of a student's grade—these points cannot be made up even if a student's absence is otherwise "allowed."

- Allow travel time when scheduling for breaks and returning from breaks so that the student doesn't have to miss classes to get a great fare on a ticket. Looking at the overall investment in education the savings of a few hundred dollars in travel costs over the course of a degree is not worth the potential impact on a grade or GPA—a GPA below a B or 3 GPA average can negatively impact a student's job search.

- If weather at certain times of the year is likely to affect travel, take this into account when planning days needed to travel to and from school; assist students in returning to school before the first day of scheduled class.

Note to students
What to do if you really need to miss class

- Not all professors will care—still, give them the courtesy of an email when you need to be out sick, or are in an accident.

- Don't expect a professor to care if your sibling/best friend/parent is getting married during the semester—missing class for any social reason is frowned upon, not excused—the best you can do is offer to make up missed work.

- Keep in touch with your faculty while you are gone—if you do have to miss class, email and be specific about when you will return.

- When you return, go to the professor's office hours and discuss the work you missed and what the professor expects from you.

- If you miss a test/exam/presentation realize you may not be able to make it up.

- If a funeral of a close family member requires you to miss a class, try to talk to the professor(s), before you leave, about making up work you will miss.

- If you cannot talk to a professor before you leave, email the professor and politely inform them of the death in your family (professors hear this very often—don't be surprised if they are skeptical) and let them know specifically when you will return to class.

School-related Travel

Some schools will allow a student, particularly a junior or senior, to miss a day of class in order to attend professional conferences, or job interviews. As mentioned in Chapter 6, professors often intentionally try to provide these kinds of experiences for students. This does not mean that a student can "disappear" from his other classes for a conference or job interview; communication needs to be maintained with a student's remaining faculty. Students should notify each of their professors before a professional absence such as a conference or interview and bring their professors documentation. This may mean bringing the professor a copy of a conference listing, or copy of an email offering a job interview. It is also a good idea to remind each professor before a student leaves that an absence is due to professional development.

Note to students

Some professors rely strictly on policy and regardless of why you miss class will tell you that the work cannot be made up—that they allow for absences by dropping the lowest grade on tests/assignments or otherwise accounting for some missed work during the semester. Review the syllabus a professor has given you (or made available online.) The syllabus almost always has a written statement about the attendance policy a professor has. Realize, however, that even professors who have a policy informing you that no work can be made up, usually appreciate knowing you are missing class for professional reasons and not because you do not value what they are teaching.

Encouraging Polite, Professional Communication

Young people, with their limited experience of professional social interactions, are still learning the value of polite, professional communication. Parents can be tremendously helpful to their children by modeling this kind of behavior/communication when dealing with others.

If a family wants their student to value education, then the parents are best served by living that value. A family should not be surprised if their student does not do well in university if they have not previously witnessed actions from their parents that show the parents value education. How, then, can a family show that they value education? When your child is still living at home and attending school, families can make time to attend parent–teacher conferences. When speaking of teachers, parents can be respectful. If the child and a teacher are in conflict, parents can assist in seeking resolution without participating in or encouraging negative conversations about school, education, or teachers.

If a family is home schooling, parents can regularly discuss the value of education in opening new opportunities to a person. Parents need to be honest and also positive. It can be helpful to discuss with students that college is a challenging time but is a chance for discovering—virtually everyone meets at least one person in college whose ideas they find engaging, interesting, and worth exploring further (they may meet the person in person or in a book—but they would not have encountered that person and their ideas without attending college.) Children may also want to know why parents expect them to attend university when up until that point the child has been home schooled. Explain that university degrees offer professional validation which will open doors to career opportunities a person otherwise would find closed.

Families can also recognize and act on the fact that school alone cannot prepare any student for college. Chapters 1 and 2 provide specific actions a family can take to better prepare their student for success in college; in summary, families need to provide the education in practical self-reliance before a student will be able to function away from home. Failure to prepare a student for the transition to being more autonomous will usually result in the student having a negative college experience.

Avoiding bullying behavior

When a student has difficulty in college, a family should avoid resorting to threats towards administrative school officials. It is also not a good idea to try bullying a student—this is usually counter-productive, which I will discuss further in a moment. My colleagues and I have all had conversations with parents who threaten us with lawyers or their close personal associations with the President of our school, members of our Board of Governors, or otherwise think they can force us to take an action the parent desires. I am not aware of either myself or anyone I work with having ever been motivated to act based on such a threat—this probably has something to do with the fact that we are aware of the law and make a point of not violating it—we are, however, often motivated to act by a family or student's requests for assistance.

We've also all worked with students who have parents threatening to punish them if they do not do better in classes. Bullying behavior is not effective in obtaining productive long-term outcomes. Most often, when a student is not following through on what she needs to do, it is because she is feeling overwhelmed. Threatening her is not likely to lead to long-term resolution of this situation; making an overwhelmed student feel more stressed usually backfires on a family. If for example a student suggests she needs to drop one class to do well in her remaining classes, reminding her of the money the family has spent might lead her to keep all the classes—and then fail one or more of these classes. Her GPA will be negatively impacted, she may be placed on academic probation, and she will be under even greater stress to do better in the following semester. This in turn is likely to cause a chain reaction of stress, trouble sleeping, and continuing declining grades.

It can also aid a student when his parents recognize that he may benefit from counseling once he is under the stress of transitioning to college. Parents can facilitate the use of counseling services by initially making sure the student knows where the center is located. A family member can walk their student to the on-campus counseling center when they initially visit campus or during moving in. Some counseling centers even provide tours during orientation week, which would be an excellent opportunity for families to discover something about the center together. Most invisibly disabled students find the greatest challenge is taking part in new experiences while feeling alone and stressed. Knowing where the counseling center is before a student needs this service can be very helpful to a student.

Parents can also check with their insurance carrier to see if off-campus counseling will be a covered benefit if their student should need this resource. It is generally a good idea for a family to check how their health benefits will impact their child's ability to seek medical treatment near their campus, before the student has moved. Remember that many STEM schools will not be in the same state/ province/district that the family lives in and some service providers outside a family's geographic region may or may not be able to accept the insurance a family uses. It is also a good idea to allow time to look for service providers who accept the family insurance *before* a student needs medical care.

Note to Parents

These are some things that you can do to assist your student:

- Encourage your student to seek out the academic support that is available on his/her campus; this works best if, when you initially brought your son or daughter to campus, you made sure to physically visit these locations with him/her.

- Take time to make sure your child has met their disability service provider—encourage your child to talk directly to this person, rather than trying to speak on your child's behalf in this meeting.

- Remind your child of the value of speaking directly to professors when they do not understand what is happening in class.

- Help your child formulate specific questions for the professor.

- Encourage your child to work on a problem/formula as far as she can and when she is stuck, to bring questions to the learning center, professor, or class teaching assistant.

- If your child continues to struggle with speaking to others, realize he may need to return to a local community college where you can offer more direct support for at least one semester and possibly for at least one academic year.

Remember that neither your child nor the professor will be able to give you as regular grade/progress reports as you had during high school. Graded work is usually given much less frequently and professors consider it the student's responsibility to keep track of their grades. Legally, professors cannot share information with parents the way high school teachers could.

The Importance of Housing Staff to Families

Of course, some children simply are not good at maintaining communication with family. Parents may become concerned during the course of the semester because a student is not responding to phone calls or emails. Parents may begin to worry about what is "really going on."

Note to Students

I cannot emphasize enough the importance of staying in touch with your parents so you don't have university employees doing regular "wellness checks" on you—which can be a little embarrassing if you are perfectly fine but forgot to call home...

One of the reasons that universities require freshmen to live on campus is so that university staff can assist new students in their transition to living away from home. Students being on campus allows the university to provide some oversight of the students' physical wellbeing as they make this important transition from being children in their parent's home, to being independent adults who are able to function on their own. University employees who work with this group of young people realize only too well that while legally they are now adults, emotionally and practically they are still maturing. Very few freshmen students arrive prepared to be completely independent. University administrators also believe that living in a structured housing environment on campus provides students many opportunities to learn social skills during their freshman year. The people responsible for so much of a student's first-year experience are the dedicated professionals who work in the Housing Department. People may not realize but Housing is an independent department staffed by professionals who have chosen a career that allows them to assist young people in reaching their potential.

When families become very concerned because they are not able to get a response from their student, or when families are concerned because every indication they have leads them to believe their student is becoming depressed or having trouble carrying out day-to-day functions, the staff who work in Housing may be some of the most important people the family can work with.

- Housing staff are professionals who specialize in helping young people successfully transition into independent adults.

- Each hall or floor has a residential advisor (RA) who is a student, who is at least at the sophomore level; these young people have been carefully selected and trained to help their peers with the transition to university; RAs work directly with professional staff.

- Housing can be contacted when a family is concerned about their child.

- Parents can request a wellness check on their student—the RA or a professional staff member will personally check in with the student and make a report on how the student seems.

- Housing can assist a student in making their way to a medical clinic or counselor if this intervention is warranted.

- Housing staff can assist a student in finding learning centers, advisors, disability service providers, and professor's offices.

- Due to their daily interaction with students, the Housing Department is often a good first place to contact when a family suspects their student is struggling with daily living, attending class, depression, eating, or leaving her room.

I work very regularly with my colleagues in the Housing Department. I am always impressed not only by their professionalism but also by their enthusiasm for the work with students that they do.

It is not uncommon for me to request a wellness check on a student after parents have contacted me concerned because their student is not responding to attempts by the parents to contact the child. Recently I had a very distraught mother who had been trying for over a week to speak to her son. He was not answering his cell phone. She had become concerned that he was lying in bed, too distressed to function. Within an hour of making the request that the student be checked on, my Housing colleagues were able to assure me this was not the case. The young man was not in his room, his backpack with books were gone indicating he had gone to class. His phone, however, had been left behind. Sometimes students get so caught up in the daily demands of college life that they will begin to neglect checking in with their family. Rather than immediately making travel arrangements to personally check on a student, family can call the Housing staff and may very well receive reassurance that the student in question is functioning in a reasonable fashion. And if a student does need assistance, Housing staff are present and ready to assist with any immediate needs.

Note to Students
When to Call Your Parents

Students—no one in the world is going to be as invested in your future as your family. These are the people who have watched you grow up and who have dedicated a great deal of their own time, energy, and resources into helping you achieve the many things you have achieved by the time you arrive on a college campus. They may know as well as you know yourself what helps you learn and what obstacles get in the way of you learning. It makes sense that these are the people in the best position to give you advice about how you can learn to adapt to your new environment and who will be the most willing to listen to you when you need someone to listen to your point of view. Just remember, if you make everything sound hopeless in one phone call, your family will hold on to that impression long after you've moved on; you may be eating pizza with friends while your parents are convinced you're huddled in a ball on your dorm-room floor. When you then forget to call home and check in don't be surprised if your family thinks this is due to a further emotional crisis on your part.

It is a good idea for families and their students to agree before the beginning of a semester how often the student will be expected to check in via email or phone. A specific plan can be modified as the semester goes on; however, it provides a starting point with clear expectations that everyone understands.

Students need to understand the importance of check-in times to their families; however, if these calls are becoming too regular and interfering with the student's study time, then the student needs to be able to explain this to their family and *renegotiate* how often they will check in. Parents in turn need to balance their own need for reassurance that all is well, with their student's need for both independence and a balanced schedule that allows for study and socializing.

Students should also realize the importance of being responsible about letting their family know how they are—an email or phone call once a week is usually considered the minimum contact a family needs to feel their student is safe and healthy. Students should try to remember, no matter how mature they become, their parents will continue to have concerns about their welfare.

It is also helpful when a student makes a point of having at least one positive thing to share with their family each week; if one focuses on the negative aspects of life do not be surprised when parents think it would be better to move or transfer to another university. This isn't to say a student should avoid sharing their struggles or discouragement. Rather, help parents keep these trials and tribulations in perspective; tell them the plan for overcoming a current obstacle or ask for their advice, so that they feel they are assisting with a productive outcome. Consider saying something like, "Does it sound like there's something I should be doing differently?" or "Have I run into this kind of problem before and if so, how did you help me get through it?"

Most of all, students, try to remember that a family listens for a balanced picture of student life—the good, the bad, the funny, and the frustrating. Students who focus too much on telling their families about just one aspect of life will probably have families that start to worry about their student and about whether a lifestyle/location change is necessary.

Note to Parents
When to Step Back
Parents, you've given the advice you have been asked for, you've taught your child for 17 years or more, and you have lived an example that has deeply affected your son or daughter. The next part of helping your child become an independent adult is helping them start to separate from you and make independent decisions…which will also bear consequences.

Families need to realize—their student may need to fail a class, or a semester, to begin to comprehend the responsibilities of life as an adult, and that their choices have consequences.

Parents need to think about this potential need for failure before a student is registered in an expensive STEM university. If having a student fail is financially problematic, or if a family has doubts that their child is ready to go directly to a STEM university, then the student should be started at a local community college or regional school—a student can always transfer after one or two years.

And yet one more reminder, parents, that a child needs to practice being an adult before he will be ready for the transition to independent living. Don't intervene in all a student's communication with authority figures in their university life; practice sitting back and letting the student speak for herself during meetings with disability service providers, the registrar's office, etc. I know it can be far easier to do something for a student than it is sometimes to watch them painfully and slowly make their way through a process. It may be necessary to repeat the mantra, "I'm training my child to be an adult, I'm training my child to be an adult…"

For example, I meet many parents who take on the task of filling out their student's housing application. Do not do this. Make the student responsible for filling out her own housing application—even if that means sitting next to her and encouraging her as she does this. A more mature family member may need to remind the student about any medical needs she has which will impact her housing application, including if a single room is necessary, refrigeration for medical supplies if needed, and discard bin for medical waste if required. Since the student may be new to this help her learn by assisting her to do—don't just step in and do for the student who needs the practice being more independent. *Each student needs to learn to self-advocate.*

Parents can assist their student as he generates a list of people he needs to speak to once he's on campus, including academic advisor, disability support staff, and his dorm RA. Students do benefit from a more mature viewpoint when it comes to creating action lists. With high rates of stress and anxiety, invisibly disabled students also benefit from having a family member present with them when they initially encounter a new environment—like their new campus. It is thus a good idea to walk a student around campus when he first arrives so he knows where to find things, and he isn't overwhelmed by all the new places and people.

This initial introduction to campus is also a good time to practice taking public transportation downtown together. Parents can also assist a student by making sure she has been to a local store and pharmacy and can find whatever basic necessities she will need during the semester—including the local clinic, and counseling services. Remember, one of the most important things a student needs from their family once away from home is emotional support. When a student calls home to complain, vent, or otherwise voice frustration, be a listener first—don't offer to solve a problem unless a family member's intervention really is necessary. It is better if a parent talks the student through the problem and helps her realize how she can take steps to solve the problem independently then it is for mom or dad to jump in and try to solve the problem for her.

Of course, it is important to let a student know that just because he is out of sight doesn't mean he has lost family support and well wishes. A care package at least once a semester is always very welcome—many universities even offer programs where parents can order seasonal goods or "study packs" for students during exam times. Learn to listen to the difference between frustrated and really overwhelmed. Even though they are growing up, students will continue to use their family as a "dumping ground" for concerns because family provides a sympathetic ear—learn to hear frustration for what it is and remember that the student who could be enemies with a person one minute and friends the next, is not necessarily dwelling on the horrible injustice they complained about several days previously.

Of course, it is always possible that a student will be too overwhelmed to function—when grades are far below normal and a student starts to sound defeated, it is possible that the move to university has been too much, too quickly. At a time like this, parents can help by reminding their student of options that are open, including trying a different school for a while, repeating classes for a better grade, and exploring other majors. Families may need to reassure their student that a discouraging class or semester is a common experience and the student may need assistance talking through what can be changed in the future so that such discouraging experiences are not repeated.

If a family reaches the point where the consensus is that the student needs professional help—career advice, counseling, disability support—the student's family members are usually the very best people to help the student receive this assistance. Parents usually know their young adults as well as any person can know another;

administrative professionals at university are going to take parent concerns seriously and will assist a family that is concerned their student is in crisis.

In some respects the young woman who sat across from me at my desk looked much the same as she had the first day we met over three years earlier. Her hair was still a little wild, looking freshly windblown as it always did; her glasses looked a little smudged, while her hands danced in the air as she explained her latest plans. When we'd first started working together she had been an undergraduate who was in danger of being permanently dismissed from school.

She summarized her mini-lecture to me, "So that's the project we'll be submitting to NASA for research."

"That's amazing," I said beaming.

"Dan thinks we'll get it," she said, referring to the professor who was now her graduate advisor—she was just in her first semester of graduate work and already planning a project for NASA.

"Oh," she added, "for this," she vaguely waved a hand in the direction of a paper about a scholarship, "Will you be able to write a letter of recommendation for me? I figure that way I cover all my bases. I have Dan for research, Julie for academics, and you as my mentor. I figure you can talk about what I'm *really* like."

Her struggles, successes and failures were fairly well known to me and I continued to be impressed by her determination; this young woman had learned to focus her considerable energy on specific goals and could make things happen. "Let me make sure I have the countries right," I said reaching for a pen and paper. "Last summer you took your language classes in Spain but I always mix up which country in South America you went to when you were designing your bridge…"

She'd done a senior design project that meant volunteering to live in a region of South America for part of the summer, designing a bridge whose parts could be carried through mountainous terrain and built by local people with local equipment. It had been a challenging project and, as always, she had risen to the challenge.

This young woman is one of the people who is responsible for me loving the work I get to do. All she'd really needed to be successful was some encouragement and practical advice along the way. Over the years we'd talked about how to set up a study environment and different strategies for studying; she'd vented about professors who "didn't understand" and I'd listened—then we discussed why sometimes you have to work with people who just don't understand; she'd started a women's sports team on campus and I had agreed to be the faculty/staff advisor. She was amazing and yet this simple fact had been lost for years to some people due to her inability to organize or focus. She'd learned so much about managing these things over the years, in large part because she was always willing to work hard and would often listen to advice—not always—but often. Like so many of my colleagues who work in STEM education, I find it a privilege to work with such amazing young people.

There are moments when I realize a young person that I am working with is not yet ready to be at a competitive STEM university. Even in those moments though, I cannot stop from thinking about how far we have come with educating people with differences. There was a time—as little as five years ago—when students would not have come as far as they now are able to proceed. The future will provide more opportunities for brilliant young people who may take longer to learn social and/or organizational skills—an increasing number of people are beginning to see the value to society that these bright young minds have to offer. It is important for each person who struggles in school despite their intellect to remember, no one yet knows what their potential or future will be. Invisibly disabled students are still creating and discovering their places in the world and it is up to each individual to decide what challenges are worthy of his or her efforts.

Glossary

Autism spectrum disorder: Autism is now being recognized as having a range of impacts, differently affecting individuals—it is thus now referred to as autism spectrum disorder, and it is now more common to say someone is "on the spectrum" rather than "autistic." Mental health policy in the US is moving towards removing the diagnostic term Asperger Syndrome (and "high-functioning autism") in favor of the inclusive use of autism spectrum disorder (ASD.) This is not a popular idea with the majority of individuals who self-identify as having Asperger Syndrome.

Academic Advisor: A professional member of staff, or a professor, who is familiar with the requirements a student needs to meet in order to graduate with a degree in a specific field. Some large departments (engineering) will have full-time academic advisors; smaller departments (philosophy, humanities) usually have a professor who also acts as an academic advisor for students within the department.

Americans with Disabilities Act (ADA): a US federal, civil rights law that protects the disabled from discrimination.

AD/HD: AD/HD is the currrent correct diagnostic term; commonly used terms are ADD or ADHD. AD/HD refers to Attention Deficit Hyperactivity Disorder, which can be made up of all/any of the three diagnostic criteria: impulsiveness; distractability; hyperactivity. This is a neurologically based discorder with a degree of genetic predisposition, i.e. it tends to run in families.

Affective disorder: A disorder which causes persistent, uncontrolled, and often unpredictable changes in a person's mood or affect; bipolar disorder, depression and unipolar disorder all fall within the affective disorder range.

Anxiety disorder: The common term for what is clinically often referred to as generalized anxiety disorder (GAD); the presence of constant worry and tension even when there is little or no reason for concern. Similar to having the "flight" response when there is no immediate threat to one's wellbeing, anxiety disorder has a more physical impact than the more common level of "worrying" that people experience—people who live with anxiety disorder are likely to develop panic attacks and/or obsessive compulsive behaviors in the face of any actual stress.

Bipolar disorder: A brain disorder, also known as manic depression. A person living with bipolar disorder will experience manic and depressive episodes (violent ups and downs) with behavior ranging from hyperactivity to an inability to function in daily life.

Chancellor: Usually the highest ranking administrator on a university campus; some campuses have a Dean of Students and not a Chancellor.

Dean of Students: One of the highest ranking administrative staff members on campus (see also "Chancellor" above.)

Discussion Board: An online (web) environment where people share ideas, opinions, and questions, usually related to a very specific topic area, for example, foods that help the brain focus.

Dyslexia: A language-processing disorder which can affect a person's ability to "read" symbols including letters and numbers; dyslexia affects individuals differently and some people who live with dyslexia are still primarily visual learners.

Early Intervention Team (EIT): At Michigan Tech University, the EIT group meets weekly when classes are in session to discuss students who for any reason have been brought to the attention of someone on the team. A team member is then assigned to follow up and further assess how best to assist the student. Different campuses may have different names for a group with a similar function.

Family Education Rights and Privacy Act (FERPA): a US federal law that protects the privacy of educational records.

Fibromyalgia: A chronic pain condition; some research is now indicating a person's brain may be amplifying pain response rather than providing "normal" levels of response to sensory stimuli.

Grade Point Average (GPA): Schools have different methods of arriving at grades for students; a student's GPA provides a more universal way of comparing grades between institutions. The student's GPA is also used as a measure of success within a school, and by lending institutions to judge the progress a student is making towards a degree.

Invisible disability: Refers to disabilities which cannot be as easily observed as the "visible" disabilities like blindness, wheelchair use, or presence of someone who is signing in response to deafness.

ISBN: This stands for International Standard Book Number. The ISBN uniquely identifies one commercially available book from another; this number is located near the front of a book on the page which includes the publisher's information. On a textbook the ISBN is also located over the bar code on the book's back cover; many professors will include the ISBN for a book on their syllabus to assist students in finding the correct edition of the book.

Learning center: A physical meeting space on campus where students can make appointments to meet with staff who are trained to work in particular areas of study such as math, English, chemistry, etc.

Learning disability: Although this term is used to generally signify someone who has any type of disability which impacts their learning there is also a category of disability known as "Learning disability—not otherwise specified" or LDNOS—which is also abbreviated as "LD."

Obsessive compulsive behaviors: Actions, often repetitive, which even if they begin out of necessity (turning off the stove, brushing teeth) are compulsively repeated; the person repeating the activity often finds that the repetition of the activity provides temporary relief from feelings of extreme anxiety.

Obsessive compulsive disorder (OCD): All functioning people have a level of "obsessive" behavior—like wanting, or not wanting, to brush their teeth every morning. An individual reaches the level of this becoming a compulsive disorder when it interferes with their daily functions: needing to wash hands multiple times in a row; becoming anxious because the tins on a shelf are not in alphabetical order—OCD behavior can take almost limitless forms.

Resident Advisor (RA): A student who lives in university housing and is employed by the Housing Department to provide some level of supervision/ leadership to other students; students are usually divided into units such as halls, floors, or houses and will have one RA in charge of each unit.

Rehabilitation Act (1973): A US federal law that prohibits discrimination in federally funded programs on the basis of a person's disability.

Scantron: Forms that can be fed through a computer for tabulation of results (users fill in small circles with a pencil.) These forms are popular for use in tests, particularly when the class includes many students. As a result, many tests will require a student to choose from multiple answers and fill in the appropriate circle on the Scantron sheet.

Smartpen: One of several products from the "Livescribe" company; contains a computer chip which will record audio in a room while the writer also takes notes. Both audio and the written notes can then be downloaded to a computer.

STEM: This stands for science, technology, engineering, and math; a school which specializes in these fields is called a STEM school.

Syllabus: The document a professor makes available at the beginning of the semester which outlines class expectations/grading policy, states the professor's office room number, office hours, and the primary assignments for the semester; some professors will also include a breakdown of the reading and assignments due each class day of the semester. A syllabus is a form of contract between the professor and the student—the professor sets out her expectations and by remaining in the class the student agrees to accept these conditions as the basis for the grade he will earn.

Teaching Assistant (TA): A non-professor who assists a professor, most commonly a graduate student in the professor's department who is basically an apprentice professor.

Tutor: A tutor is someone who has a strong enough background in a subject that they are able to assist someone who is learning the subject matter; a tutor may be a paid professional, a same-age peer, or a volunteer.

Index